GETTING THE
PICTURE

Nancy Herzfeld-Pipkin
American Language Institute
San Diego State University

GETTING THE PICTURE

Everyday Listening/Speaking with Idioms

Heinle & Heinle Publishers
A Division of Wadsworth, Inc.
Boston, Massachusetts 02116 U.S.A.

Photo Credits (by page number)
 2: Paul Conklin, Monkmeyer Press
11: Hugh Rogers, Monkmeyer Press
21: Dan Chidester, The Image Works
31: Ursula Markus, Photo Researchers
41, 73, 96, 109: Joel Gordon, Joel Gordon Photography
64: Mimi Forsyth, Monkmeyer Press
85: Lehtikuva Oy, Woodfin Camp

Publisher: Stanley J. Galek
Editorial Director: David C. Lee
Assistant Editor: Ken Mattsson
Project Management: Hockett Editorial Service
Editorial Production Manager: Elizabeth Holthaus
Production Editor: Kristin M. Thalheimer
Manufacturing Coordinator: Jerry Christopher
Interior Art: David Weisman
Interior and Cover Design: Marsha Cohen, Parellelogram

Getting the Picture: Everyday Listening/Speaking with Idioms

Heinle & Heinle Publishers is a division of Wadsworth, Inc.

Manufactured in the United States of America

Library of Congress Cataloging-in-Publication Data

Herzfeld-Pipkin, Nancy, 1951–
    Getting the picture : everyday listening/speaking with idioms /
Nancy Herzfeld-Pipkin.
        p.   cm.
    ISBN 0-8384-2667-0
    1. English language—Textbooks for foreign speakers.   2. English
language—Conversation and phrase books.   3. English language—
-Spoken English.   4. English language—Idioms.   5. Listening.
I. Title.
PE1128.H4353   1991
428.3′4—dc20   91-47866
                                                                                         CIP

10 9 8 7 6

Contents

LESSON 11 ....

At the Airport: A Close Call   109

(a close call/as a last resort/at the last minute/at (time) sharp/
  count on someone/no matter what/one at a time/
  see someone about/under the circumstances)

LESSON 12 ....

Review: Lessons 7–11   120

Teacher's Script   129

Glossary   160

Preface

Getting the Picture: Everyday Listening/Speaking with Idioms is designed to be used with intermediate-level students in ESL or EFL classes at the college/university, adult, or secondary levels.

This text was written with several goals in mind:

- to familiarize students with common idioms in English
- to present and practice these idioms in real-life/everyday contexts
- to provide extensive listening and speaking practice with these new expressions
- to provide students with active involvement in the learning process throughout each lesson
- to enhance cultural awareness through the topics/contexts presented

The book consists of 12 lessons, 2 of which provide review. Each lesson presents no more than 9 new idioms, so as not to overwhelm students with too many new expressions at one time. The bulk of each lesson is made up of exercises/activities that afford students as much active involvement as possible. Many of these provide listening and speaking practice.

A wide variety of contexts has been incorporated into the lessons in order to familiarize students with typical situations encountered by native speakers and/or students studying in English-speaking countries. These situations/contexts have not been limited to conversations or dialogues as is often the case in idiom texts. The exercises and activities in this text include (but are not limited to) the following: public announcements and notices, short narratives, telephone messages, excerpts of sports broadcasts, informal conversations, business conversations, sample newspaper clippings, business presentations, and simple instructions. In addition, some lessons focus on the practice of idioms through typical functions such as getting/giving directions and making/refusing invitations.

Each of the 10 lessons providing new material is divided into eight sections. These sections have been organized to take the students from more controlled exercises/activities to more open-ended ones. Following is a list of these sections in the order in which they are presented. Each one has been given a title expressing the intent of that section:

Getting Your Feet Wet
Getting the Picture
Figuring It Out
Learning the Ins and Outs

Catching On
Holding Your Own
Wrapping It Up
Talking It Over

The exercises/activities in the two review chapters include crossword puzzles, more listening practice, dictation, problem solving, games, and group story telling.

To augment the listening component of this text, an accompanying cassette tape is available. All of the listening exercises as well as many of the other exercises in the text are included on this tape. (Tapescripts of the listening exercises for each lesson have also been included at the back of the text—see Teacher's Script. In this way, instructors who do not have access to the tape can provide the listening exercises themselves.) In addition, other listening and pronunciation exercises have been provided on the tape. These exercises include practice with reduced forms, contractions, intonation, and distinguishing between specific sounds.

It is hoped that this book will have a wide range of appeal to teachers and students. Students who may be studying English for their own personal growth, as well as those who are learning it for more academic purposes, should be able to benefit from this book.

Acknowledgments ....

I would like to thank all my friends and colleagues who were very supportive of me during the writing of this book. Many of them were so positive and encouraging that they really kept me going. In particular, I want to thank Roseanne Mendoza, who was always a pleasure to work with, for helping me during the early stages of this text. I also want to thank my students, who through the years have made teaching not only enjoyable but exciting, enriching, and enlightening for me as well.

I would also like to thank the following reviewers, who provided valuable commentary during the development of the manuscript: Donna Jurich, San Francisco State University, San Francisco, CA; Barbara Francesdini, Experiment in International Living, Brattleboro, VT; and Mary Horosco, Florida International University, Miami, FL.

I must also say a special thank you to several family members: my husband, Jack, and my boys, Seth and Scot, for enduring days, nights, and weekends of watching me on the computer; and my mother, Evelyn Herzfeld, and my brother, Gerry, for always being there when I need them.

Finally, this book is dedicated to the memory of my wonderful father, Paul Herzfeld, always a source of inspiration to me.

Nancy Herzfeld-Pipkin

To the Teacher

Getting the Picture: Everyday Listening/Speaking with Idioms presents and provides practice with 87 common idioms for intermediate-level students of English. Ten lessons present eight or nine new idioms each, and two chapters review five lessons each. Most of the exercises/activities in this book deal with typical, everyday situations, and many of them provide listening and/or speaking practice. A cassette tape of many of these exercises is available. Scripts for all listening exercises are provided at the end of the text for those teachers who do not have access to the tape.

The following descriptions and suggestions are meant to help the teacher understand the organization of the text and provide specific ideas on how to utilize it.

General Notes about Exercises/Activities in This Book......................

There are 10 lessons which present new idioms. Each of these lessons is divided into eight sections, which progress from more structured, controlled exercises to more creative, open-ended activities.

- Many of the exercises in this book have more than one possible answer.
  - In the case of the multiple-choice exercises, the directions explicitly tell students to look for more than one possible answer.
  - In the fill-in exercises, students are told that more than one idiom may fit a space.
  - In the less structured exercises within the "Holding Your Own" and "Wrapping It Up" sections, many answers will of course be possible.

  These types of exercises have been included to show students that many variations are possible in language. It is hoped that this will help them when dealing with English outside the classroom, where they may encounter such variations. It is also hoped that this approach will help students really use and manipulate the language themselves.

- Most of the exercises/activities in this book lend themselves well to pair or small group work. More specific information on this is given in the discussion of chapter organization below.
- Examples are given for a few exercises. For those exercises where no example has been given, the teacher might want to do the first one or two ques-

tions with the class as a whole, to be sure students understand exactly how to complete the exercise.

Following is a more detailed description of all the sections, and suggestions on how to present or follow up on them.

Chapter Organization ....

GETTING YOUR FEET WET

This section introduces the topic of the lesson either through discussion or an activity. In some lessons, students are asked to discuss various cultural issues. In other lessons, students are given tasks, such as filling out a form, giving directions to someone, making invitations, etc. Some of these tasks involve listening activities as well. Most of these discussions or activities can be done in pairs, in small groups, or with the class as a whole. In some cases the students must do the given task on an individual basis.

A photograph has also been included in this section of each lesson. Whenever possible, the photo should serve as another vehicle for eliciting discussion as a preview of the chapter.

After the introductory discussion or activity is completed, the new idioms are introduced in this section. In some of the lessons, they are presented in a short conversation. In other lessons, they are introduced through short narratives (such as the tour guide/registration information), an advertisement, different accounts of an accident, and parts of a televised sportscast. If the tape is available, students should listen to this section with their books closed. Later, some students may want to act out the situation for speaking practice. If the tape is not available, the teacher may call on students to read the conversations, or the teacher may read this section to the class.

GETTING THE PICTURE

This section includes comprehension questions to be sure students understand the general meaning of the introduction. After the students hear the introduction of the new idioms in the first section, they should go over these questions. For more listening practice, or with a more advanced group, the teacher may want to do these questions orally (with books closed) as well. It is hoped that some of the meanings of the new idioms will be elicited during the discussion of these questions. In this way, this section works as a "lead-in" for the next part ("Figuring It Out"), where the students will work on finding the meaning of each idiom introduced in the chapter.

FIGURING IT OUT

These inductive exercises ask students to discern the meanings of the new idioms. In some cases the students are given a list of meanings and then asked to match them with the idioms found in sentences. Students should refer to the introduction (in "Getting Your Feet Wet") as well as to the sentences in this exercise, so they can see how the expression is used in more than one context. It is often very helpful to have students do these exercises in pairs or small groups before the instructor goes over the answers with the class as a whole. Answers to these exercises should be discussed before going on to the "Catching On" section, since that section asks students to go beyond the meanings and be able to recognize how to use the idioms.

In other cases no meanings are given, and students must try to guess the meanings on their own. This type of exercise has been included in order to give students practice in the very important skill of context guessing. This type of exercise mimics "real life" in the sense that students must work toward finding the meanings of new expressions on their own, just as they would when dealing with native speakers outside the classroom. Again, students should refer to the introduction (in "Getting Your Feet Wet") as well to the sentences in this exercise, so they can see how the expression is used in more than one context. It is also very possible that some meanings have already been discussed in the "Getting the Picture" section. It is highly suggested that students do such exercises in pairs or small groups. Then, it is particularly important for the instructor to go over the answers with the class as a whole to be sure that students understand the meaning of each new expression.

Note: The teacher may want to stress to the class that this exercise is meant to help them figure out meanings on their own. If the students get frustrated by one or two that they can't figure out, they should be encouraged to skip those and do the others. Then when the exercise is discussed with the class as a whole, they will get the meanings. The exercise that follows this type (in the "Catching On" section) always goes over the meanings of the new expressions to be sure that students clearly see the meanings.

A Note About Meanings

Meanings of the new idioms can be found in several places in this text.

- Some of the exercises in the "Figuring It Out" section provide the meanings as choices, for answers.
- If the exercise in the "Figuring It Out" section does not provide meanings as choices, the "Catching On" section will go over the meanings.
- The Glossary at the back of this volume provides a list of all the idioms introduced in this text. Both meanings and lesson numbers are provided in this section. This list is intended as a reference. Students should be encouraged to work out the meanings from the exercises, rather than refer to the Glossary!

LEARNING THE INS AND OUTS

This section primarily provides information on usage. This section is not intended to provide meanings for each of the new idioms. This is the only section of the lesson that does not ask students to complete an exercise or activity. Instead, extra information, usually other than the idiom's meaning, is given for those idioms that might be confusing to students. In some cases, students are shown how to use the "separable" idioms with both nouns and pronouns.

CATCHING ON

This section presents two exercises:

1. The first exercise provides a review of the meanings or uses of the new idioms. If no meanings were provided in the "Figuring It Out" section, this exercise reviews the meanings through matching or multiple-choice exercises. If meanings were provided in the "Figuring It Out" section, this exercise asks students to show how they can use the new expressions through multiple-choice or finding the response exercises. All of these exercises can be done individually or in pairs or small groups.
2. The second part of this section is always a listening exercise. Students are given listening practice through a variety of activities. In some lessons, students hear a sentence and then must choose an appropriate response to the statement. In other lessons, students listen to two statements (one with a new idiom and one without) and must decide whether they have the same meaning. Other activities in this section include listening to short dialogues and answering questions about them or listening to short announcements, presentations, or narratives and then identifying the idioms heard and answering questions about their content. One lesson asks students to take telephone messages as well.

It is best to have the cassette tape available for these exercises, so that students can hear a variety of voices. It may be necessary to play the tape two times for these exercises, depending on the level of the students. If the tape is not available, the instructor can use the tapescripts at the back of the text instead.

HOLDING YOUR OWN

This section also presents two exercises:

1. Most of the exercises in this section are the fill-in-the-blank type. In some cases, students must fill in parts of conversations. In other cases they must complete notices, short newspaper articles, or short stories. The purpose of these exercises is to give students more practice in using

the new idioms in different contexts through a rather controlled/ structured activity.

2. The second part of this section presents a less controlled exercise. In these exercises, students must write sentences or questions to fit a particular situation or conversation. Often the students are asked to use a given idiom in these exercises, but in a few cases they choose the idiom they feel would be most appropriate.

Both of the exercises in this section lend themselves well to pair or small group work.

WRAPPING IT UP

The activities in this section ask students to be more creative and independent. In many of the lessons, students must work with a partner or in a small group in order to complete the activity. In all of these activities, the students must use as many of the idioms from the lesson as possible. (Students are not given specific idioms to be used in this section.)

Activities in this section include:

- creating dialogues for specific situations
- writing sentences that would be appropriate for specific situations
- telling stories about given illustrations
- information gap activities (i.e., creating conversations with specific roles given to each partner/giving directions with a specific map)

As follow-up to these activities, teachers may want to do the following:

- Have some students share their answers orally with the class
- Have some pairs or groups role-play their answers for the class
- Have students complete their answers in writing for the teacher to correct

TALKING IT OVER

In this final section, students are asked to have some free discussion, using the idioms from the lesson. These questions may be discussed in pairs or small groups and then with the class as a whole, or just with the class as a whole. Teachers may want to have students do these questions in groups and then report back to the class, or they may want students to write their answers and hand them in for the teacher to correct.

Review Lessons ·······························

There are two review lessons as follows:

Lesson 6: reviews lessons 1–5
Lesson 12: reviews lessons 7–11.

As in the other lessons within the text, each review lesson begins with more structured, controlled exercises and progresses to more creative, open-ended ones.

Each review lesson has nine exercises:

- The first two exercises are crossword puzzles. Crossword puzzles lend themselves well to pair work.
- The next two exercises review meanings of the idioms through matching and choosing the expression with a different meaning.
- Exercise five provides listening practice by asking students to answer specific questions using suggested idioms. Students should be encouraged to try to give as many different answers as possible (using different idioms) in this part.
- Exercise six is a dictation and answer activity. Each dictation question contains an idiom being reviewed. After the students write the question, they must also answer the question, using one of the idioms given. Again, students might be encouraged to give as many answers as possible.
- The seventh exercise is a problem solving activity. Students are given a specific situation and asked to write down both problems and solutions, using as many of the given expressions as possible.
- The eighth activity is an "Idiom Game Show." This activity works very well as a group or team activity, since students often like the "competition." The teacher may want to modify some of the instructions, depending on the group. Following are some possible variations for this activity:
  - If one person/team cannot answer a question, another team might be given the chance to answer and get the points.
  - If a person/team answers incorrectly, points may be deducted from the total score.
  - If the person/team gives the correct idiom, but does not make grammatical changes necessary to fit the sentence, partial points may be given.
  - If students wish to play individually, all questions can be played on the tape (or read by the teacher), and then all answers reviewed at the end. The person with the highest total score wins.
- The final activity in the review lessons is a "Story Go 'Round." This gives each student a chance to contribute to a story about an illustration in the book. The story can change direction at any time, depending on how each student chooses to answer at his/her turn. If this activity is too difficult for a particular group of students, the class could be divided into small groups/pairs and each pair or group can make up its own story. Then the stories should be shared with the class as a whole, possibly through role-plays.
- Another possible activity that has not been spelled out in the review lessons could be a kind of "telephone" game. In this case, a student would come up with a sentence using one of the idioms being reviewed. (Sentences from some of the exercises in the book could be used.) Then the students would play the game of telephone, whispering the sentence from

person to person, in an attempt to preserve the original sentence until the last person.

Cassette Tape ....

The accompanying cassette tape can be used with any of the exercises that have been recorded. The tape should be used for the listening exercises in each lesson. Various other exercises in the text have been included on the tape. For the most part, exercises on the tape come from the following sections of the book: "Getting Your Feet Wet," "Getting the Picture," "Catching On," and "Holding Your Own." The exercises from the "Catching On" and "Holding Your Own" sections include the answers. For this reason, students should listen to them after they have completed and gone over those exercises first. The "Idiom Game Show" from each review section has been provided on the tape for those teachers who wish to use it. In this case, students will not be able to pick and choose the questions, but must do all of the questions in the order given on the tape. This symbol [▭] can be found throughout the text, and it indicates which exercises are on the tape.

In addition to the exercises in the book that are on the tape, there is an additional section on the tape at the end of each lesson. This section is called "More Listening/Pronunciation Practice" and consists of three parts as follows:

- Listen and Repeat—this section provides pronunciation practice of the new idioms. Students will hear the speaker on the tape say the new expressions. Then the students will repeat them.
- Listening—this part asks students to listen for specific words, forms, sounds, or intonation. Some of the exercises in this part ask students to listen for specific words or forms (such as reduced forms found in conversation) and to write them down. In other exercises, students must refer back to parts of the introduction in the "Getting Your Feet Wet" section. Other exercises ask students to identify sounds they hear in sentences taken from parts of the lesson. Whenever necessary, sentences for these exercises are provided in the "Teacher's Scripts" section at the back of the text. If some sentences in these exercises are too long for lower-level students, teachers may want to have the students do each sentence in parts, rather than all at once.
- Pronunciation—in this part, students will be asked to pronounce various words and forms that were focused on in the previous section. In the case of reduced forms, some teachers may wish to have students practice saying these forms out loud. Others may not feel completely comfortable with this; therefore, it should be optional. At the very least, though, students should be familiar with these forms so that they can recognize them in conversation with native speakers, thereby aiding in their listening comprehension.

Teacher's Script ·····································

Tapescripts for all listening exercises can be found at the back of the book. These have been provided for those teachers who do not have access to the tape and for those teachers who may wish to go over some of the material with the students after the listening exercises have been completed. This section includes the script for all of the "More Listening/Pronunciation Practice" sections as well. As mentioned above, some exercises in the "Listening" section of the "More Listening/Pronunciation Practice" require the students to complete exercises that have been provided in the scripts. (More specifically, these exercises are found in the scripts for Lessons 5, 8, and 10.)

Glossary ·····································

A glossary of all the idioms introduced in this book has been provided at the back of this volume. The idioms have been listed in alphabetical order and lesson numbers have also been given in parentheses. (A list of idioms for each lesson has also been provided in the Table of Contents.) As discussed above, this list is provided as a reference only. Students should be encouraged to find the meanings through the exercises in this book.

To the Student

This book is called *Getting the Picture: Everyday Listening/Speaking with Idioms*. What is an idiom? An idiom is a special expression. It can be two words, three words, four words or more. The words in an idiom work together to have a special meaning. Look at the title of this book. What does "getting the picture" mean? Does the meaning of each word in this expression tell you the meaning of the idiom?

"Getting the picture" is an idiom that means to understand the general meaning or to understand the situation in general. If you try to find the meaning of this expression in the dictionary, you will probably have trouble. This is because the dictionary will give you the meaning of each word in the idiom, but it will probably not tell you the meaning of the whole expression. This book will help you learn many idioms, so that you can "get the picture" when you use English, especially with native speakers.

In this book you will find many exercises and activities to help you understand and use many idioms. Through these exercises and activities you will also be practicing your listening and speaking skills. Each lesson has eight parts. Each part has a title with an idiom. These titles tell you the purpose of that section of the lesson. Here are the titles you will see and their meanings:

Getting Your Feet Wet   beginning something or having your first experience with something

Getting Your Feet Wet	beginning something or having your first experience with something
Getting the Picture	understanding the whole situation or general idea
Figuring It Out	studying something to find an answer or explanation
Learning the Ins and Outs	learning how to do something; learning the details
Catching On	getting the meaning; beginning to understand well
Holding Your Own	being able to do well; maintaining yourself
Wrapping It Up	finishing
Talking it Over	discussing

Finally, try to listen for the expressions in this book and practice using them as much as possible!

LESSON 1
Registration: Taking Care of Business

Getting Your Feet Wet ....

Registration and application forms are very common in schools or businesses. Lisa is a new student and must complete the form below. Listen to Lisa give information about herself and then complete the form for her. Write the information in the correct spaces on this form.

REGISTRATION INFORMATION

Name_____
                family name   first   middle

Address_____
           street address

_____
    city   state/country   zip code

Phone Number_____
              area code   number

Sex   F   M   Birthdate _____ / _____ / _____
                            month   day   year

You are going to take a two-week class for managers, and you have just arrived at the school to begin the course. Listen as registration begins.

Good morning, everyone. My name is Edna Monroe, and **I am in charge of** today's registration. Before we begin, I have some instructions and announcements for you. Please listen carefully to them. Then I will try to **clear up** any questions you may have.

To complete today's registration, you will need to do two things. First, you must see Mr. Bils at the desk in the front of the room and **hand in** all of your papers. Please be sure to **fill out** these forms carefully. Then, you will see

1

Mrs. Wong at the computer so that you can **take care of** payment for the course. Some of you have paid **in advance.** You must still see Mrs. Wong, so that she can make sure your account is completely **up-to-date. As a rule,** we prefer payment in cash or by personal check. Please speak to Mrs. Wong if you have a question about this.

There is one change in the schedule for this afternoon. The 2:00 P.M. class will meet in Room 16, *not* in Room 10. I have written this information on the blackboard behind me. Please **make a note of** this change.

Now, if you have completed all of your papers, please see Mr. Bils. You may form a line at his desk. Does anyone have any questions?

Getting the Picture..

1. Where does this situation take place?
2. What should the people at this registration do first?
3. What should these people do next?
4. Is it necessary to see Mrs. Wong? Why or why not?
5. How should someone pay for this course? What kind of problem could a person have with making a payment?
6. What is the schedule change for this afternoon?
7. Who should see Mr. Bils first?

Figuring It Out...

In each sentence below you will find one of the idioms in the registration information Ms. Monroe gave above. You will also find a list of meanings below. Look at how each idiom is used in the information above and in the sentence in this exercise. Find the meaning that matches each idiom. Then try to think of another meaning or synonym for as many of these idioms as possible.

MEANINGS

- (be) responsible for
- give attention to
- usually

- explain/fix (a problem)
- before
- write down

- give (to someone)
- current/the latest
- complete (a form or other paper)

1. Please **fill out** this application to get your new credit card.

   another meaning _____

2. **As a rule,** Jeremy doesn't eat cake or ice cream, but today he is having both.

   another meaning _____

3. I'm going to the library to do my report. I need **up-to-date** information about this sub-ject, and all my books at home are too old.

   another meaning _____

4. If you have any questions, please see Gary. He's **in charge of** this program and he has all the answers.

   another meaning _____

5. I'm sorry about the problem you had yesterday, sir. I'll talk to the manager and see how to **clear up** the mistake.

   another meaning _____

6. Friday is the last day to **hand in** your reports to the boss; please be sure to finish them as soon as possible.

   another meaning _____

7. That telephone number has been changed. Please **make a note of** the new telephone number: 457-1128.

   another meaning _____

8. I paid for my hotel room **in advance,** so now I'll just pay for the telephone calls I made.

    another meaning _____

9. My parents went to a restaurant for dinner tonight, so I have to **take care of** my little brother.

    another meaning _____

Learning the Ins and Outs ....

Three of the idioms from this lesson can be expressed in two ways by changing the position of the second word. Look at the following examples:

> **hand in** something/**hand** something **in**
> Examples: I'll **hand in** the paper tomorrow.
>   I'll **hand** the paper **in** tomorrow.
>   I'll **hand** it **in** tomorrow.

> **clear up** something/**clear** something **up**
> Examples: He should **clear up** the problem as soon as possible.
>   He should **clear** the problem **up** as soon as possible.
>   He should **clear** it **up** as soon as possible.

> **fill out** something/**fill** something **out**
> Examples: You must **fill out** all of these papers immediately.
>   You must **fill** all of these papers **out** immediately.
>   You must **fill** them **out** immediately.

In the examples above, how does the position of the second word in the idiom change? Does the meaning of the sentence change when this happens? There are other two-word idioms in English that can be used this way. You will find some of them in other lessons in this book.

In the last example for each idiom above, what kind of word do you find between the two words of the idiom? Remember that when a pronoun (me/ you/it/her/him/us/them) is used with these idioms, it **must** go between the two words. A pronoun **cannot** be placed after the second word of the idiom.

> Examples: Correct: You must fill **them** out immediately.
>   (Incorrect: You must fill out **them** immediately.)

Catching On ....

FIND THE RESPONSE

Next to each number in the column on the left you will find the beginning of a conversation. Next to each letter in the column on the right you will find some responses. Find the response on the right that fits each sentence or question on the left. Choose the letter of the correct answer. Write the letter next to the number on the left.

_____ 1. Should we make hotel reservations in advance?

_____ 2. Are you sure this report is due next week, and not this week?

_____ 3. It's time to go now. Please give me all of your papers.

_____ 4. Ms. Woo is going to be in charge of your group's project.

_____ 5. I thought you bought a new computer. Where is it?

_____ 6. Class is over now. Do I have everyone's assignment?

_____ 7. I'm going out dancing with Carlos tonight. He's such a good dancer.

_____ 8. Did you see my friend Sue when you returned the toaster yesterday?

_____ 9. As a rule, I don't like to stay out too late on a weeknight.

a. Yes. I made a note of the date during the last meeting.

b. Oh that's great! I'd love to work with her.

c. It's back at the store. They are trying to clear up a problem with it.

d. No. I haven't handed mine in yet. Can I bring it tomorrow?

e. I know. He always knows the most up-to-date steps.

f. But today's your birthday. We should go out tonight to celebrate!

g. Yes, we have to. That's a very popular place this time of year.

h. Yes, she took care of the problem. Thanks for helping me with it.

i. I haven't filled out the last form yet. May I give it to you later?

LISTENING

You are going to listen to several short conversations. After each one, you will hear a question. Find the best answer for each question. Circle the letter of your answer.

Part A

1. a. the man
   b. Mrs. Rubino
   c. Ms. Winston

2. a. She wants Andrea to go out with her.
   b. She wants Andrea to take her child out.
   c. She wants Andrea to watch her child.

3. a. He already gave the order to the cook.
   b. The cook never changes an order.
   c. He has already given the man his food.

4. a. a very modern one
   b. an old one
   c. a used one that is on sale

5. a. He always lets his workers leave early.
   b. He only lets his workers leave early to go to the airport.
   c. He usually doesn't let his workers leave early.

Part B

1. a.   She wants to hand in a problem.
    b.   She wants to clear up a problem.
    c.   She wants to fill out a problem.

2. a.   She had to register as a rule.
    b.   She had to register up-to-date.
    c.   She had to register in advance.

3. a.   She must fill out the paper.
    b.   She must hand in the paper.
    c.   She must clear up the paper.

4. a.   He didn't fill out the papers for it.
    b.   He didn't make a note of it.
    c.   He didn't ask about it in advance.

Holding Your Own..

Below you will find two notices with blank spaces. Fill in each of the blanks
with one of the idioms below. You will not use all of the idioms, and you should
not use any idiom more than one time. More than one answer may be correct
for some of the blank spaces.

•in charge of	•clear up	•in advance
•up-to-date	•hand in	•fill out
•make a note of	•take care of	•as a rule

COMPANY PICNIC NOTICE

 This year's company picnic will take place on Saturday, June 15 at Lake Murray

Park. Be sure to _____ this date on your calendar. There will be

food, games, and lots of fun.

 If you plan to attend this picnic, please _____ the attached paper to let

us know you are coming. You should _____ this paper to the Personnel

Department by June 10. Tina Rodriguez is _____ the food and

games. If you can help her, please talk to her as soon as possible.

 See you at the picnic!

> ### CLASS CANCELLED
>
> **Date:**   Monday, January 11
>
> **Time:**   9:00–10:00 A.M.
>
> **Instructions:**   The test on Chapter 1 will be given on Wednesday. If you cannot take this
> test, you *must* speak to the instructor _____ . Be sure you are _____
> on all assignments. Call or see Ms. Piret in her office to _____ any questions or
> problems. She will be in her office on Tuesday from 1:00–3:00 P.M.

WHAT'S THE QUESTION?

Complete each conversation below by making a question that will fit the answer given. Be sure to use the idiom given in parentheses in your question and to change it to agree with the rest of the sentence if necessary.

1. **A:** _____?

   (in charge of)

   B: I'm not sure. I think it's Mr. Ross, but it might be Mrs. Johnston.

2. **A:** _____?

   (clear up)

   B: It's a pretty big problem. I hope we can solve it before next week.

3. **A:** _____?

   (hand in)

   B: I never accept late papers. Please have your work ready tomorrow.

4. **A:** _____?

   (take care of)

   B: Don't worry. John will go to the store and buy all the food.

5. A: _____?

    (in advance)

    B: Yes. If you pay now, it costs $10. If you buy it at the door, it will be $15.

6. A: _____?

    (up-to-date)

    B: No, it isn't. We moved last month; the new address is 15 Main Street.

7. A: _____?

    (as a rule)

    B: Yes. Usually I go to the fitness center at least three times a week.

8. A: _____?

    (make a note of)

    B: I sure can. Here's an appointment card for your next visit to the doctor.

9. A: _____?

    (fill out)

    B: Yes, we need that information on all of those papers.

Wrapping It Up ....

Your teacher will assign you a partner or group. Together you will choose one of the situations below and create a conversation about it. Be sure to use as many idioms from this lesson as possible in your dialogue. Be prepared to share your work with the class.

SITUATIONS
•••••••••••••••••

1. You have had a charge card for the past five years and you have been an excellent customer. You always pay your bills on time. A few weeks ago, you received a bill that said you were late for a payment. You called the company and were told it was a mistake. Today, you received another late bill from this company. This bill also has an extra late charge. This means that

now you must pay even more. Now you are calling the company to find out what is happening.

2. Six months ago you moved to a new house. Since then, you have been receiving mail for the family who lived in that house before you moved there. You have told the post office several times about the change, but you continue to receive mail for the other people. Now you are at the post office trying to explain the situation. You do not want to receive the wrong mail anymore.

Talking It Over...

1. Have you ever been in charge of anything at work, school, or home? What was it? Was it a difficult thing to take care of? What were the difficulties you had?
2. What kinds of things do you usually do in advance when you are taking a trip?
3. As a rule, do you hand in your work for school or job early, at the right time, or late? Would you like to change this? Why or why not?

LESSON 2

At a Restaurant: What Do You Feel Like Eating?

Getting Your Feet Wet ....

1. What is your favorite kind of restaurant?
2. When you eat at a restaurant, what kinds of foods do you usually order?
3. What do you order when you don't have very much money?
4. What time do people usually eat dinner in your country? What time is an early dinner or a late dinner?
5. Look at the photo on the next page. What do you see? What do you think these people are talking about?

Lois and Sam are old friends, and they haven't seen each other in a while. They have just arrived at the restaurant where they will eat dinner tonight. They are trying to decide what to order.

LOIS: This menu has so many choices. I just can't **make up my mind.**

SAM: Well, what do you **feel like** eating? Do you want some steak or roast beef?

LOIS: **To tell you the truth,** those dinners are too expensive. I had to fix my car last week and now I'm almost **broke.**

SAM: **That makes two of us.** I have to buy a new refrigerator. A steak dinner is **out of the question** for me.

LOIS: What time is it? There's an **early bird special** until 6 o'clock. You get chicken, rice, a vegetable, and coffee for only $6.99.

SAM: It's 6 o'clock right now. Do you think we can still get it?

LOIS: I don't know. We can **find out** from the waitress. Here she comes now.

10

Getting the Picture...

1. Why is it difficult for Lois to decide what to order?
2. Does Sam have any suggestions?
3. Why doesn't Lois want to choose Sam's suggestions?
4. Do you think Lois and Sam brought much money with them to the restaurant? Why or why not?
5. Do you think Sam might possibly choose the steak dinner? Why or why not?
6. Why does Lois want to know the time?
7. What will Lois and Sam ask the waitress?

Figuring It Out..

In each sentence below you will find one of the idioms from the conversation. Look at how each idiom is used in the conversation and in the sentence in this exercise. Then try to guess the meaning of each idiom. Write the meaning on the line below each sentence.

1. That ice cream store has 35 flavors. John can't **make up his mind** about the kind he wants.

   make up one's mind (about) _____

2. Janet is very tired tonight so she doesn't **feel like** cooking dinner.

   *feel like*_____

3. Bill: Would you like to go to the movies with me tonight, Karen?

   Karen: **To tell you the truth,** Bill, I'd love to go but I can't. I have to stay home with my little brother tonight.

   *to tell you the truth*_____

4. Mahmoud just bought an expensive new boat. He can't buy a new car now because he **is broke.**

   be broke _____

5. Cindy: I'd like to learn how to play tennis.

   Sally: **That makes two of us.** Maybe we can take a class together.

   that makes two of us _____

6. Andreas had a skiing accident and broke his leg. Now it is **out of the question** for Andreas to ski next weekend.

   be out of the question _____

7. Some restaurants have **early bird specials** for breakfast in the very early morning hours.

   early bird special _____

8. I have to get Maria at the airport tonight but I don't know what time her plane is arriving. I'll call the airport and **find out.**

   find out _____

Learning the Ins and Outs.............................

feel like

Be sure to put "ing" on the verb that follows this idiom.

Examples: What do you feel like **doing** tonight?
I feel like **watching** some television.

This idiom is usually used in less formal situations or in situations that are not so serious.

Example: Your friend wants to go bowling but you do not. You can say, "I don't feel like bowling today."

Sometimes it can be considered rude to use this idiom in more serious or formal situations.

Example: Your teacher asks for your homework and you did not do it. It may not be very polite to say, "I didn't feel like doing my homework."

make up one's mind

Be sure to change the possessive **one's** to match the subject when you use this idiom. Notice how this changes in the following:

I made up **my** mind last night.
You made up **your** mind last night.
She made up **her** mind last night.
Ben made up **his** mind last night.
We made up **our** minds last night.
Those people made up **their** minds last night.

This idiom can be expressed in two ways by changing the position of the word **up** in the sentence.

Examples: Which shirt will Bob buy?
I don't know; he can't **make up** his mind.
I don't know; he can't **make** his mind **up.**

out of the question

Use this idiom only in definite or strong situations to show that something is impossible. Do not use it when you want to say "probably not."

find out

This idiom is only used for information. Do not use it to say that you found something you lost.

early bird special

This expression is most often used for meals served at special times at a restaurant. Sometimes it can be used for special sales in other businesses.

that makes two of us
> Be sure to use this expression when you want to say you agree with someone else's opinion or situation.

Catching On...

CHOOSE THE MEANING

Choose the letter of the word or expression that has the same meaning as the italicized idiom in the sentence. In some cases more than one answer may be correct.

1. Marcia wants to take a vacation. She will call her travel agent to *find out* about a trip to Mexico.
    a.   get the information
    b.   tell someone
    c.   remember

2. I want to see a movie tonight. What do you *feel like doing?*
    a.   have to do
    b.   want to do
    c.   prefer to do

3. It was closing time at the store. The saleslady told Roberta to *make up her mind* about the new dress.
    a.   think
    b.   decide
    c.   forget

4. Petra has to write a big report for her boss. Going to the beach with her friends is *out of the question* today.
    a.   a good idea
    b.   possible
    c.   impossible

5. When Jenny said she was very hungry, her friend said, *"That makes two of us.* Let's get some food."
    a.   I don't agree.
    b.   I feel the same way.
    c.   I agree.

6. Antonio's mother wanted to know why the living room window was broken. Antonio said, *"To tell you the truth,* I broke it when I was playing baseball this afternoon."
    a.   honestly
    b.   frankly
    c.   surely

7. Dave and Sue will have dinner at 4:00 P.M. tonight because they want the *early bird special* at the new restaurant down the street.
   a. special chicken dinner
   b. inexpensive meal served at certain times
   c. new kind of unusual food

8. Sam can't buy a present for his wife because he *is broke*.
   a. doesn't know what she wants
   b. doesn't want to give her a present
   c. doesn't have any money

 LISTENING

Listen to the statements. Then look at the choices next to each number to find an answer that fits with the statement you heard. In some cases only one answer may be correct. In other cases two choices may be correct. Circle the letter(s) of the correct answer(s).

Part A

1. a. Isabella's brother doesn't usually tell the truth.
   b. Isabella's brother was probably broke.
   c. Isabella's brother gave her an honest answer.

2. a. Bettina has been buying that magazine for a long time.
   b. Bettina probably wants to order the magazine because it's less expensive for her.
   c. Bettina will not order the magazine at all.

3. a. Maybe Bill must work this weekend.
   b. Maybe Bill's car needs many repairs.
   c. Maybe Bill is going to Miami this weekend.

4. a. Bob spent all of his money.
   b. Bob broke his television.
   c. Bob probably went to the bank today.

5. a. Oliver doesn't like the new car, but his wife loves it.
   b. Oliver and his wife have the same opinion about the new car.
   c. Oliver's wife doesn't like the new car, but Oliver does.

Part B

1. a. She probably feels like playing tennis.
   b. She probably doesn't feel like doing anything.
   c. She feels like resting and sleeping today.

2. a. Sandy can make up her mind tomorrow.
    b. Sandy should make up her mind immediately.
    c. Sandy is trying to make up her mind right now.

3. a. He should find the price of a car at a car dealer.
    b. He should find out the price of a car at a car dealer.
    c. He should find out where he can buy an inexpensive car.

4. a. He probably bought the early bird special.
    b. It was probably too late for the early bird special.
    c. The early bird special was probably more expensive than other things.

5. a. It is out of the question for Minoru to take the subway home now.
    b. Taking a bus home is out of the question.
    c. Taking the subway home is not out of the question.

Holding Your Own...

Fill in each blank in the following conversation with one of the idioms listed below. You will use some of the idioms more than once. Be sure to make any necessary changes in the idiom to agree with the rest of the sentence.

- make up one's mind
- that makes two of us
- early bird special

- to tell you the truth
- out of the question
- find out

- feel like
- be broke

HELEN'S CHECKUP

Helen Conners is at her doctor's office. They are talking about the results of her annual checkup exam.

HELEN: So how am I doing, Dr. Garcia?

DR. GARCIA: All your test results are fine, Helen. But _____ you gained a little too much weight this past year.

HELEN: I know. I never _____ dieting, but I always _____ eating.

DR. GARCIA: You don't have to diet to lose weight. Why don't you _____ about joining a health club or fitness center?

HELEN: I guess a regular exercise program would be good for me, but I'm afraid that's _____. Those places are so expensive.

DR. GARCIA: Last week another patient told me about a new center on Elm Street. It just opened, and they're having a(n) _____ _____. If you join during the first month, you'll get a special price!

HELEN: That sounds interesting, but I _____ this month. I bought a new house last month, and I've been buying lots of new furniture.

DR. GARCIA: Well, you need to _____ about what's most important to you. I'd like to see you a little thinner at next year's checkup.

HELEN: _____. Maybe I should _____ about that new fitness center.

ARRIVING AT THE HOTEL

A tourist has just arrived in a city he has never visited before. Right now he is registering at his hotel. He is talking to the clerk at the desk. On the next page you will find parts of their conversation. On each line, you should complete the sentence or write a sentence to fit the conversation. Be sure to use the idiom in parentheses in each of your answers. Remember to change the idiom to fit the sentence if necessary.

1. TOURIST: I had such a long train ride to get here. I'm so tired now.

    CLERK: _____

    (that makes two of us) Note: Be sure to write more than just the idiom for this
    one.

2. TOURIST: _____
    (feel like)
    Is there an inexpensive restaurant nearby?

    CLERK: We do have a restaurant in this hotel, and _____

    _____
    (early bird special)

3. CLERK: Have you decided how long you will be staying with us?

    TOURIST: _____

    _____
    (to tell you the truth) (make up one's mind)

4. TOURIST: Do I have cable television and movies in my room?

    CLERK: Just a moment, please. _____
                                        (find out)
    That costs an extra $10 a night. Would you like to take it?

    TOURIST: No thanks. _____
                            (out of the question)

    _____
    (be broke)

Wrapping It Up ....

Read each situation below. Then write an answer to each question. Use one of
the idioms we studied in this lesson in each of your answers. Each answer
should be a complete sentence. Be sure to use each idiom at least one time.

1. Your friend wants to go to Disneyland next Saturday. You would like to go, but you don't

    have much money right now. What will you tell your friend?

    _____

    _____

2. You are at a travel agency, and you are trying to decide where to go for your vacation next month. The travel agent has just given you information about New York, Rio de Janeiro, and Paris. Now she wants to know your decision. What will you tell her?

_____

_____

3. You and a friend have just finished eating dinner at a restaurant. The food was very good, but the service wasn't. Your waiter was not very helpful and was very slow. You are talking with your friend about the tip for the waiter. What might you say to your friend?

_____

_____

4. You and your best friend have just seen a movie. It's 10:00 P.M. and you are discussing what to do now. You each have a suggestion about what to do. What are your suggestions? (Try to give two different suggestions.)

Your Suggestion:_____

_____

Your Friend's Suggestion: _____

_____

5. Your son/daughter just got his/her driver's license yesterday. S/he wants to drive your new car to school today. What will you tell him/her?

_____

_____

6. You want to buy your girlfriend/boyfriend a birthday gift. You go to a jewelry store, and the salesperson shows you an expensive ring, an inexpensive watch, and a gold necklace. You're not sure if you want any of these things. What are two things you can say to the salesperson?

A. _____

_____

B.   _____

      _____

7.   You are downtown in a big city with a friend. It's 4:00 P.M. and you are both hungry. You
     find a restaurant on the corner and you see a menu in the window. You look at the menu
     and talk about eating there. What might you and your friend say to each other about the
     menu or the restaurant? (Give two separate sentences.)

     You: _____

     _____

     Your Friend: _____

     _____

Talking It Over ....

1.   Have you ever been broke or almost broke? Imagine that you are a visitor
     in your native city or the city you are now living in, and you have very lit-
     tle money. What could you see and do without spending much money?
2.   When you are preparing for a trip to another country or city, what kinds
     of things should you find out about before you leave? What specific things
     did you have to find out about before your trip to the United States?
3.   What kind of tipping customs do you have in your country? Is tipping out
     of the question in some places? Do you tip only when you feel like it?
     Compare tipping customs in your native city or country to the city where
     you are living now for the following places or situations:
     • at a cheaper (or fast food) restaurant
     • at a better (more expensive) restaurant
     • at a bar
     • at a gas station
     • in a taxi
     • at your home when someone is delivering something (for example, new
       furniture or a pizza)
     • at a beauty shop or barber (for example, getting a haircut)

LESSON 3

An Accident: Pay Attention to the Road

Getting Your Feet Wet...

 Look at the picture below. Study it for 10 seconds. Try to remember as many details as possible. Then turn to the next page and listen to the questions. Answer the questions in the spaces provided on the next page. Do not look back at the picture when you answer the questions.

 An accident has just happened at this corner. Three witnesses have described the accident to the police. Here are the statements of the three witnesses.

WITNESS 1:   I saw the truck coming down College Avenue. **Right away I** noticed it was traveling too fast. **In fact,** I heard someone yell to the driver to slow down. Then, just as the yellow light was turning red, he started to go faster. **All of a sudden,** I heard a big crash. I guess the driver of the blue car didn't see the truck speeding up at the intersection. When the car started to make a left turn, it went right into the truck.

WITNESS 2:   I don't think the driver of the car **has a leg to stand on.** The truck came through the intersection on a yellow light. It didn't turn red until he crossed the street. But the driver of the car **jumped the gun** on the left turn signal. He turned before his light turned green!

WITNESS 3:   **I feel sorry for** the driver of the car. He waited for the green light to make his left turn. He was **taking it easy** going through the intersection and BANG! Just then the truck came flying across the road. The driver of the truck wasn't **paying attention to** the changing light. I sure hope he has good insurance.

Getting the Picture..

1. What kind of accident was this? (Who or what was involved in this accident?)
2. Do all of the witnesses have the same story? What do you think is the reason for this?
3. Which vehicle was witness #1 watching?
4. Why do you think the driver of the truck went faster when the light was yellow?
5. What did witness #2 think about the driver of the truck? What did this witness think about the driver of the car?
6. What did witness #3 think about the driver of the car?
7. Why does witness #3 hope the driver of the truck has good insurance?

Getting Your Feet Wet—Answers.....................

1. _____

2. _____

3. _____

4. _____

5. _____

Figuring It Out...

In each sentence below you will find one of the idioms from the story about the accident. You will also find a list of meanings below. Look at how each idiom is used in the story above and in the sentence in this exercise. Find the meaning that matches each idiom. Then try to think of another meaning or synonym for as many of these idioms as possible.

MEANINGS

• actually	• pity	• look at/listen to carefully	• start before the correct time
• go slowly	• immediately	• not have a good story	• without warning

1. Yoshi has to be at work in fifteen minutes and he can't be late. He should leave his apartment **right away.**

    another meaning _____

2. Maria is new to this country. **In fact,** she just arrived here last week.

    another meaning _____

3. The baby was sleeping quietly for over an hour. Then, **all of a sudden** he woke up and started to cry.

    another meaning _____

4. Carol's parents heard her come home after midnight last night. She says she was home at 11:00 P.M., but she **doesn't have a leg to stand on.**

    another meaning _____

5. The runners began the race but had to stop and return to the starting line. One of the runners had **jumped the gun** before it was time to begin.

    another meaning _____

6. Ben is getting a divorce and he also just lost his job. I really **feel sorry for** him.

    another meaning _____

7. It's starting to snow and the highway is getting very dangerous. You should **take it easy** driving on this road.

    another meaning _____

8. If you want to learn how to make this delicious cake, **pay attention to** your mother while she is making it.

another meaning _____

Learning the Ins and Outs ....

not have a leg to stand on
> Remember to use this idiom in the negative. This means you will need to add the auxiliary do (do/does/did).
> Example: Jim **didn't have a leg to stand on** when he told his wife he lost all his money in Las Vegas.
> This idiom is used when someone does not have a good reason or excuse for a problem.
> Example: Jim **didn't have a leg to stand on** when he told his wife he lost all his money in Las Vegas.
> (Problem: Jim lost all his money. Excuse: gambling in Las Vegas. His wife will probably think this is not a good reason to lose money.)

jump the gun
> This idiom is often used with sports because a race or sporting event often begins with the shot of a gun. This expression is sometimes used in other cases when someone starts something before the correct time.

in fact
> This idiom is usually used when you want to add extra information. Do not use it to repeat the same information.
> Example: Did George buy a new car? Yes, **in fact** he bought an expensive sports car.
> **DO NOT SAY:** Yes, in fact he bought a new car.

feel sorry for someone/something
> This expression should be used when you pity someone or something. It is not used when you feel sorry about a situation.
> Examples: That cat has a broken leg. **I feel sorry for** it.
> Ben has a broken leg. **I feel sorry for** him.
> **DO NOT SAY:** I just lost my money and I feel sorry for that.

all of a sudden
> This idiom is used to say that something happened quickly. It
> shows that one situation changes quickly to something else.
> Example: I was walking through the woods and every-
>   thing was very quiet. Then, **all of a sudden**
>   a large bird flew out of a tree and scared me.

take it easy
> In this lesson you learned that this idiom means to go slowly. It
> can also mean "to relax."
> Example: A: Where are you going for your vacation?
>   B: I'm not going anywhere. I've decided to stay
>   home for a week and **take it easy.**

Catching On..

USING THE IDIOMS

Complete each statement by choosing from the **a, b, c** choices. Circle the letter of your answer.

1.   Gerry feels sorry for his friend. Gerry's friend probably
     a.   just won a lot of money.
     b.   had an accident with his car.
     c.   got some very good news.

2.   Lisa has been sick all week. She shouldn't go to work today. She should
     a.   take it easy.
     b.   jump the gun.
     c.   pay attention to work.

3.   I need a copy of this report as soon as possible. Can you copy it
     a.   in fact?
     b.   all of a sudden?
     c.   right away?

4.   Betty needs to pay attention to the instructions for the test. Betty should
     a.   pay money in order to get the instructions.
     b.   give some money to the people giving the test.
     c.   listen carefully to the instructions.

5.   Alexis thought she was getting a raise, so she bought a present for herself.
     Then she found out she did not get a raise. Alexis
     a.   jumped the gun.
     b.   took it easy.
     c.   paid attention.

6. The boss is out sick today.
    a. Right away, it's the third time this month.
    b. In fact, it's the third time this month.
    c. All of a sudden, it's the third time this month.

7. I was driving on the freeway, and all of a sudden I heard a strange noise. I
    a. heard the noise the whole time I was driving.
    b. only heard the noise before I got on the freeway.
    c. was surprised when I heard the noise.

8. Jim went to a party last night, so he didn't study for the test. Then he failed the test. He
    a. doesn't have a leg to stand on.
    b. has a leg to stand on.
    c. paid attention to the test.

 LISTENING

After each number, you will hear two sentences, A and B. In each case, one sentence will contain one of the idioms from this lesson. In some cases the two sentences will have the same meaning, and in other cases they will not. Listen carefully. Then circle the word "same" if you think the sentences have the same meaning, or "different" if you think they do not have the same meaning. You will be listening for the general meaning. The two sentences do not have to be EXACTLY the same.

Example: Same   Different

1.   Same   Different

2.   Same   Different

3.   Same   Different

4.   Same   Different

5.   Same   Different

6.   Same   Different

7.   Same   Different

8.   Same   Different

Holding Your Own...

Below you will find a short conversation and a short story. Fill in each blank space with one of the idioms below. Use each idiom only one time.

- pay attention to
- all of a sudden
- right away
- jump the gun
- in fact
- feel sorry for
- take it easy
- (not)have a leg to stand on

THE SPEEDING TICKET

Jack has just been stopped by a police officer for driving too fast on a city street.

JACK:	I'm sorry, officer. I didn't know I was driving too fast. _____ I thought I was going right at the speed limit.
OFFICER CLARK:	I'm afraid you didn't _____ the new speed limit sign at the last corner. The limit changes on this street from 30 miles per hour to 20.
JACK:	But I didn't know that. The speed limit on these streets is usually 30.
OFFICER CLARK:	Yes it is usually, but it's different on this street because of the new elementary school over there. We want drivers to _____ around the children. You really _____ because you just drove past the sign. I'll give you a warning this time, but next time you'll get a ticket!
JACK:	Thanks, officer.

THE DRIVING TEST

Poor Paolo failed his driving test yesterday. When he first got into the car, the tester told him not to start _____. But Paolo was so nervous he _____ and drove right onto a busy street. The tester was angry and told Paolo to stop the car, so he did. _____ another car quickly came around Paolo, and the driver started to scream at him. Paolo had stopped too quickly and the other driver almost hit him! Then the tester told Paolo to go back to the motor vehicle building because he had failed the test. I _____ Paolo. Now he has to take the test again.

WHAT WOULD YOU SAY?

Complete each conversation below using the idiom given in parentheses. Each of your answers should include at least one complete sentence.

1. A: Greg, could you please take out the garbage? Our dinner guests are coming soon.

    B: _____

    (right away)

2. A: Jane, are you sure you told your brother to meet us at the movie theater at 8 o'clock?

    B: _____

    (in fact)

3. A: I just saw Gina in the park, and her clothes are all dirty. What happened?

    B: _____

    (all of a sudden)

4. A: Do you think Robert's mother will believe his story about the accident he had with her new car?

    B: _____

    (not have a leg to stand on)

5. A: I saw Joe cross the finish line first. Why didn't he win the race?

    B: _____

    (jump the gun)

6. A: Are you going to invite Enrique to the party?

    B: _____

    (feel sorry for)

7. A: Fahad has been working for several hours on that report for his boss. He wants to finish it as quickly as possible.

    B: _____

    (take it easy)

8. A: Why can't I learn this new dance?

    B: _____

    (pay attention to)

Wrapping It Up ....

WHAT'S HAPPENING?

Look at the following pictures. With your partner or group, make up a story about what's happening in these situations. Use as many idioms from this lesson as possible in this story. Be prepared to tell your story to the class.

Talking It Over ....

1. Describe a time when you did not pay attention to some instruction from a teacher or parent or boss. What was the result?
2. Describe an accident you may have had and how it happened. Try to use as many idioms from this lesson as you can in your description.
3. Have you ever given an excuse when you really didn't have a leg to stand on? Describe the situation.
4. Have you noticed a difference in the driving habits of people in your country and people in the city where you are now living? How do people drive in both of these places? Do they usually pay attention to the rules? Do they take it easy when they are driving in the big cities or on the highways? What advice might you give someone who will be driving in your native city for the first time?

LESSON 4

An Invitation: Are You in the Mood to Go Out Tonight?

Getting Your Feet Wet...

It's 4:00 P.M. on a Friday afternoon, and George Mason is finishing the day's work. He wants to go to a movie tonight, but he doesn't want to go alone. He's asking some of his friends at the office to go with him. Can you think of different ways that George can invite people to join him? Write down as many different ways as you can.

1. _____

2. _____

3. _____

4. _____

5. _____

Listen as George invites people to go out with him tonight.

GEORGE: Hey everybody, it's almost time to go home. I think I'll start the weekend by going to the movies tonight. Betty, would you like to join me?

BETTY: Oh, I couldn't tonight. My cousins from San Diego are here. They're going to **drop by** my apartment this evening. Thanks for the invitation, though. Can **I take a rain check?** Another day might be better.

GEORGE: Sure, no problem. Carmen, do you have any plans for tonight? Why don't you come with me to the science fiction festival at the Grand Theatre? Do you like science fiction?

CARMEN: No, not at all. I prefer comedies or adventure films.

GEORGE: Are you sure I can't **talk you into** coming with me?

CARMEN: No thanks, George. I'm really not **in the mood for** the movies tonight anyway.

GEORGE: What about you, Rudy? Let's go to the festival tonight.

RUDY: Sorry, George. I'm just too tired.

GEORGE: **Come on,** Rudy. Don't **turn me down** too. It'll be fun.

RUDY: I don't think so. Maybe we can go some other time.

GEORGE: Well, it's **up to you.** But if you **change your mind,** you can **get in touch with me** later. I'll be home until 8 o'clock.

Getting the Picture...

1. What does George want to do tonight?
2. Why can't Betty go with George?
3. Does Carmen want to go with George? Why or why not?
4. Why doesn't Rudy want to go?
5. What time will George go to the movies?
6. Do you think anybody will go with George tonight? Why or why not?

Figuring It Out...

In each sentence below you will find one of the idioms from the conversation. Look at how each idiom is used in the conversation and in the sentence in this exercise. Then try to guess the meaning of each idiom. Write the meaning on the line below each sentence.

1. Paula is going to buy a present for Daniel this afternoon. Maybe she will **drop by** his apartment this evening and give the present to him then.

   drop by _____

2. I'm sorry you can't go with us on our fishing trip. You can **take a raincheck** for our next trip, though.

   take a rain check _____

3. George is broke, so don't try to **talk him into** going out tonight. He'll never say yes.

   talk someone into something _____

4. That meal was delicious; now let's have some dessert. I'm **in the mood for** some pie and ice cream.

   (be) in the mood for something _____

5. I'm too tired to go out dancing now. Let's stay home tonight.
   Oh, **come on.** It'll be fun to go out. Let's just go for a little while.

   come on _____

6. Bill asked Laura to go out to dinner with him last night, but she **turned him down.** She said she was going to a party at her office.

   turn someone down _____

7. Do you think the office will close early on Monday for the holiday?
   I don't know. It's **up to the boss.** He always makes those kinds of decisions.

   (be) up to someone _____

8. What is Mary going to do this weekend?

    I don't know. First she said she was staying home and resting. Then she said she wanted

    to go to the zoo. Now she says she **changed her mind** again.

    change one's mind _____

9. You can **get in touch with me** at my new address and telephone number.

    *get in touch with someone*_____

Learning the Ins and Outs ....

drop by
    This idiom is usually used in informal situations. Often you **drop by** someplace without an invitation or without telling the people you are coming.

talk someone into something
    Be sure to put the verb that follows this expression in the "ing" form.
    Example: He talked me into **staying** for dinner at his house last night.

    This idiom means to convince someone or change another person's thinking. Remember to change the **someone** to the person who is changing his/her thinking.
    Examples: She talked **John** into going with us. (John didn't want to go with us, but she convinced John to go.)
        I talked **him** into going with me.
        I talked **them** into going with me.

change one's mind
    This idiom is used when someone changes his/her own thinking or opinion (not another person's thinking).
    Example: I wasn't planning on going to the party, but then **I changed my mind.**

Be sure to change the possessive **one's** to match the subject when you use this idiom. Notice how this changes in the following examples:

I changed **my** mind last night.

You changed **your** mind last night.

She changed **her** mind last night.

Ben changed **his** mind last night.

We changed **our** minds last night.

Those people changed **their** minds last night.

turn someone/something down—turn down someone/ something

This idiom can be expressed in two ways by changing the position of the word **down** in the sentence.

Examples: I invited him to the party but he **turned** my invitation **down.**

I invited him to the party but he **turned down** my invitation.

I invited him to the party but he **turned** me **down.**

(This idiom works in the same way as the idioms in "Learning the Ins and Outs" in Lesson 1—see page 4.)

be up to someone

This idiom means it is the decision of a particular person. Remember to change the **someone** to the person who is making the decision.

Examples: It's up to **you.**

It's up to **her/him.**

It's up to **them.**

It's up to **the boss.**

take a raincheck

This idiom can be used in different ways.

1. Sometimes it is used when someone can't accept an invitation but would like to be invited again.

2. Other times it is used in stores, especially when there is a sale. In this case, the item on sale is sold out, so the store gives the customer a piece of paper called a **raincheck.** When the store gets more of this item, the customer can return with the raincheck and buy the item for the sale price.

Catching On ....

MATCHING

Match the idioms on the left with their meanings on the right. Put the letter of the correct meaning in the space next to the number.

___ 1. drop by

___ 2. take a raincheck

___ 3. talk someone into something

___ 4. in the mood for

___ 5. come on

___ 6. turn someone down

___ 7. up to you

___ 8. change one's mind

___ 9. get in touch with someone

a. your decision

b. visit

c. communicate with someone

d. refuse/say no

e. feel like/want to

f. have a new idea or opinion

g. ask for another invitation or chance

h. say please/encourage someone

i. persuade/convince another person

LISTENING

Listen to the following statements or short conversations. Then look at the choices next to each number to find an answer that makes sense with the statements. Circle the letter of the correct answer.

Part A

1. a. Sally will send me an invitation this week.
    b. Sally told me to visit whenever I can this week.
    c. Sally doesn't really want anyone to visit her this week.

2. a. Raul is very excited because he will go to Harvard.
    b. Raul is going to Harvard now but is not sure if he will continue to go there.
    c. Raul wanted to go to Harvard, but the school did not accept him.

3. a. Carl will probably call Liz when he gets back from Los Angeles.
    b. Carl is going to be in Los Angeles for more than a week.
    c. Carl probably doesn't want to contact Liz at all when he returns from Los Angeles.

4. a. Mark gave Gary his car as soon as Gary asked for it.
    b. Gary tried to convince Mark to lend him the car.
    c. Mark told Gary he had to have the car back early.

5. a. Dr. Johns can make the decision to change the assignment date.
    b. It is impossible for anyone to change the assignment date.
    c. Dr. Johns cannot make any decisions; only the students can.

Part B

1. a. It isn't easy to change Jim's mind.
    b. It's easy to change Jim's mind.
    c. Jim probably doesn't change his mind very often.

2. a. Everyone probably took a raincheck for the game.
    b. Because it was raining, nobody could take a raincheck.
    c. All the fans stayed for the game in the rain.

3. a. Alice probably couldn't talk Charles into going to the movie.
    b. Charles wanted to go out last night, so he talked Alice into going to
        see a movie with him.
    c. Alice probably talked Charles into going to the movie.

4. a. Ilaria wasn't in the mood to eat at any restaurant last night.
    b. Ilaria was in the mood for cooking a big pizza at home last night.
    c. Ilaria wasn't in the mood to cook but wanted to eat pizza last night.

Holding Your Own..

Fill in each blank in the following conversations with one of the idioms listed
below. You should use an idiom only one time, but you will not need to use all
of the idioms. Be sure to make any necessary changes in the idiom to agree
with the rest of the sentence.

•drop by	•take a raincheck	•in the mood for
•come on	•turn someone down	•talk someone into something
•change one's mind	•up to someone	•get in touch with someone

 OFFICE TALK

Two workers are talking to each other during their coffee break.

WORKER #1:   Did you hear about Tom Hays? The boss wanted to give him a

            promotion, but Tom _____.

WORKER #2:   Why did he do that?

WORKER #1:   I don't know. The boss tried to _____ taking the new
            job, but Tom still said he didn't want it.

WORKER #2:   That's incredible. Do you think Tom will _____?

WORKER #1:   It's too late. The boss already gave the promotion to Carlos Ayala.

OLD FRIENDS

Pam Sanders is just finishing some shopping at the mall on a Saturday afternoon. As she's walking to the parking lot, she hears a man call her name.

MAN: Pam Sanders, is that you? How have you been?

PAM: I don't believe it—Peter Strauss. How are you?

PETER: It's great to see you. In fact, I tried to call you yesterday, but you weren't home. Do you have some time to talk now? Are you _____ some lunch?

PAM: I'm sorry. I was just going home.

PETER: Oh. _____. Can't you spend just a half an hour with me?

PAM: I really can't right now. I'm late. Can I _____ on that lunch?

PETER: Sure. Are you ever in the downtown area? You should _____ my office. I'd love to see you.

PAM: I'm downtown every Tuesday and Thursday. I'll be sure to _____.

PETER: Great! I hope I see you soon.

WHAT'S THE QUESTION?

Complete each conversation below by making a question that will fit the answer given. Be sure to use the idiom given in parentheses in your question and to change it to agree with the rest of the sentence if necessary.

1. A: _____?

   (get in touch with someone)

   B: No. I didn't talk to him yesterday. In fact, I haven't heard from him in more than a week.

2. A: _____?

   (in the mood for)

   B: I'd like to listen to jazz, but if you prefer rock and roll, that's okay too.

3. A: _____?

   (drop by)

   B: I'll be home after 6 o'clock tonight. Anytime after that is fine.

4. A: _____?

   (turn someone/something down)

   B: She had to go to a family dinner at her grandmother's house that night.

5. A: _____?

   (take a raincheck)

   B: Yes, you should. The store will probably be getting more of those next week.

6. A: _____?

   (up to someone)

   B: No, it's not your decision. The teacher will give you the book you need for that report.

7. A: _____?

   (change one's mind)

   B: Yes, you can. But you have to make your final decision before next Friday.

8. A: _____?

   (talk someone into something)

B: I guess he did. When I spoke to Greg, he said he wasn't going to the picnic. Then I saw him there.

9. A: _____?

(come on)

B: No, I'm sorry. I really can't go anywhere with you tonight.

Wrapping It Up ....

Read the following situation with your classmates.

SITUATION
• • • • • • • • • • • •

You and your partner are visiting New York City for the first time. You arrived yesterday, and you are only spending three days there. Today is Saturday, and you have just spent a busy day at the Metropolitan Museum of Art and at Central Park. It's almost time for dinner, and you are in your hotel room trying to decide where to go and what to do this evening.

Now your teacher will assign partners. One of you will be PARTNER A, and the other will be PARTNER B. If you are PARTNER A, read only the information under PARTNER A below and follow the instructions given. If you are PARTNER B, read only the information under PARTNER B below and follow the instructions given. Be prepared to share your conversation with the rest of the class at the end of this activity.

Partner A
• • • • • • • • • • •

You are very tired and hungry. You would like to eat at a restaurant close to the hotel and then do something quiet, such as see a movie or listen to some music at the lounge of a hotel. Below is a list of the things you would most like to do this evening:

• eat a big steak at the restaurant in your hotel
• listen to some jazz at the hotel across the street
• see a movie at a theater near the hotel
• watch a movie in your hotel room

Your partner also has a list of things s/he would like to do. Discuss with your partner what you will do tonight. Try to agree on where you will eat dinner and at least one thing you will do after dinner. Try to use as many of the idioms from this lesson as possible in your conversation.

Partner B
• • • • • • • • • • •
You are hungry and a little bit tired. You think you will probably feel much better after you eat a big dinner. You would like to eat some interesting ethnic food and then do something fun, such as go out dancing or walk around Greenwich Village, and perhaps stop in a club to listen to some music. Below is a list of the things you would most like to do this evening:

- eat in Chinatown or Little Italy
- find a lively nightclub where you can go dancing
- go to Greenwich Village and look for a club where you can listen to music

Your partner also has a list of things s/he would like to do. Discuss with your partner what you will do tonight. Try to agree on where you will eat dinner and at least one thing you will do after dinner. Try to use as many of the idioms from this lesson as possible in your conversation.

Talking It Over ....

1. Is it usual in your culture/country to drop by other people's homes? Is it polite or acceptable to visit someone without a specific invitation?
2. In your country, are there any situations where you might take a raincheck? Is this a typical practice?
3. Are some ways of turning people's invitations down more polite than others? Look back at the original conversation in this lesson and discuss the different ways that people turned George down. Can you think of any other ways to turn down an invitation politely? Can you think of any specific things you should *not* say when you want to say no politely? How do people politely turn down invitations in your country?

LESSON 5

An Advertisement: Take Advantage of This Sale

Getting Your Feet Wet ....

1. Is there much advertising on the television or radio in your country? How often do you hear or see advertisements during a radio or television program? Where else do you find advertising in your country?
2. Do you ever decide to buy something because of advertising? Has an advertisement ever changed your mind about buying a product?
3. When you shop in your country, do you look for special sales? Do you bargain for better prices? (Do you discuss the price with the salesperson to try to make it cheaper?) In what situation(s) is bargaining acceptable in your country? In what situation(s) is bargaining acceptable in the United States?

Listen to the following radio advertisement.

Is your old refrigerator **on its last legs?** Did you **pay an arm and a leg** for your television set? Is your dishwasher **a lemon?** This is Mark Shark from the Shark Discount Appliance Center, and I'm here to tell you about my incredible final closeout sale. That's right, folks. I'm **calling it quits** and leaving San Diego. Starting November 5th I'll have the lowest prices in town on refrigerators, microwaves, stoves, dishwashers and televisions. So come to Roseland Street and **take advantage of** this exciting sale. **Believe it or not,** everything in the store will be half price! And if you come with cash, we'll give you another 10 percent. **In other words,** you'll get 60 percent savings when you pay cash and 50 percent when you pay with a check or charge card. And I'm not **pulling your leg.** So don't **put off** your visit to my store. On November 5th, come to Shark Discount Appliance Center at 65 Roseland Street for my final closeout sale. You won't be sorry.

Getting the Picture...

1. What kind of store is this advertisement for?
2. Why is the owner having this big sale?
3. What kinds of things will a customer find on sale at this store?
4. What is the best discount you can get during this sale? How can you get this discount?
5. What other kind of discount can you get?
6. When will this sale start?

Figuring It Out...

In each sentence in this exercise you will find one of the idioms from the advertisement. You will also find a list of meanings below. Look at how each idiom is used in the advertisement above and in the sentence in this exercise. Find the meaning that matches each idiom. Then try to think of another meaning or synonym for as many of these idioms as possible.

MEANINGS

- give up
- in very bad condition
- postpone
- fool someone
- it's the truth
- make use of something
- spend a lot of money
- that is to say
- defective product (product that has problems as soon as you buy it)

1. I bought that refrigerator more than 20 years ago. Now it's so old that it's **on its last legs**.

    another meaning _____

2. Mark decided to go to New York last weekend. He had to **pay an arm and a leg** for his airplane ticket because he bought it the day before he went.

    another meaning _____

3. My brother bought a new car two months ago. He's going to sell it soon because it has so many problems. It's a real **lemon**.

    another meaning _____

4. Ben and Ivan played chess for several hours. Then Ben realized he couldn't win, so he **called it quits** and ended the game.

    another meaning _____

5. That airline is selling tickets to New York for only $99 each way. If you want to **take advantage of** that price, you must buy the ticket before midnight tonight.

    another meaning _____

6. What did you get on that difficult math test we had last week?

    Believe it or not, I got 100 percent!

    another meaning _____

7. This office will not be open from December 24 until January 2 for the winter holidays. **In other words,** we will be closed for 10 days starting on December 24.

    another meaning _____

8. I can't believe you're quitting your job and moving to Hawaii!

    I'm really not. I just like to **pull your leg**.

    another meaning _____

9. I wasn't able to get that new television on sale. **I put off** my shopping until Sunday, and by then the sale was over.

    another meaning _____

Learning the Ins and Outs ....

on its (one's) last legs

This idiom is most often used for things or animals. Sometimes it can be used for people as well. It is usually used for something (someone) that is in bad condition because it's (s/he is) old.

a lemon

Something is often called a lemon when it has a problem or problems even when it's new. Often a lemon can't be repaired or gets repaired and then develops a new problem. This idiom is used mostly for machines or mechanical equipment. It is commonly used for cars.

take advantage of

This idiom can mean that you can benefit or profit from something.

Example: Last winter we went to Hawaii on vacation. We
                 took advantage of the beautiful weather
                 and went to the beach every day.

Sometimes when you take advantage of something, it can be in a negative way.

Example: The taxi driver took the tourist on a long ride to
                 the hotel and charged her $50. The hotel was only
                 two miles from the airport. The taxi driver **took
                 advantage of** the tourist.

believe it or not

This idiom is usually used in a surprising situation when it is difficult to believe the truth about something. The speaker thinks that the listener might not believe what s/he is saying because the information is so unusual or surprising.

pull one's leg

When you pull someone's leg, you fool someone. Remember to change the possessive (one's) to agree with the person being fooled.

Examples: I pulled **his/her** leg at the party last night.
                   The boss was pulling **my** leg when he told me **I**
                       was fired.
                   It's easy to pull **your** leg because you believe
                       everything I say.

put off something/put something off

This idiom can be expressed in two ways by changing the position of the word **off** in the sentence.

Examples: He **put off** his studying until it was too late.
He **put** his studying **off** until it was too late.
He **put** it **off** until it was too late.
(This idiom works in the same way as the idioms in "Learning the Ins and Outs" in Lesson 1—see page 4.)

in other words
This idiom is used when you want to explain something. You are saying the same information in another way.

Catching On...

USING THE IDIOMS

Complete each statement by choosing from the **a, b, c** choices. In some cases only one choice is correct. In other cases two choices may be correct. Circle the letter(s) of your answer(s).

1. It's raining too hard to play soccer today, so they will
   a. take advantage of the weather.
   b. put off the game.
   c. pay an arm and a leg to play.

2. Those people have been working on that problem for over a decade. _____ they have been working on it for more than 10 years.
   a. In other words,
   b. Believe it or not,
   c. I'm pulling your leg;

3. Janet's old color television is on its last legs. It gets only one station in black and white now. Her television is
   a. in good condition.
   b. a big piece of furniture.
   c. in bad condition.

4. I bought an expensive watch for my husband, and I paid an arm and a leg for it. I hope he's not angry with me because I
   a. spent a lot of money.
   b. spent very little money.
   c. paid a high price.

5. Dennis said to Jack, "Believe it or not, last night I looked up in the sky and saw the planets Mars and Jupiter." Dennis thought
   a. Jack saw the planets too.
   b. Jack was pulling his leg.
   c. Jack was probably going to be surprised.

6. I have a problem. I just bought a new computer, but it's a lemon. What's my problem?
    a. It's a bad product; it doesn't work right.
    b. I can't understand how to use the computer.
    c. I paid an arm and a leg for the computer.

7. It was a difficult job to do, so I thought I should
    a. believe it or not.
    b. take advantage of it.
    c. call it quits.

8. Bob's brother said he could lend him the money for a new car. Bob will probably
    a. buy a car on its last legs.
    b. take advantage of his brother's offer.
    c. pull his brother's leg.

9. Raja is a funny guy. He likes to pull everyone's leg at the office. Raja likes to
    a. be serious with everyone.
    b. make jokes with everyone.
    c. fool everyone.

LISTENING

You are going to hear three short listening passages. The first will be a department store announcement. The other two will be a short story that will be told in two parts. You will do two things after you hear each passage:

1. In each part below you will see a list of the idioms from this lesson. Listen for any of these idioms in the passage. Put a check next to each idiom you hear in the space provided.
2. After you hear each passage, answer the questions. If necessary, you may hear the passages a second time in order to answer the questions.

Department Store Announcement

Listen to this short announcement at a department store.

____ on one's last legs   ____ pay an arm and a leg   ____ call it quits

____ take advantage of   ____ a lemon   ____ in other words

____ pulling one's leg   ____ believe it or not   ____ put something off

Questions

Answer the questions about the announcement. Circle the letter of the correct answer.

1. What time will this sale begin?
   a. 2:00 P.M.
   b. 3:00 P.M.
   c. 10:00 A.M.

2. What will be on sale?
   a. all jewelry
   b. gold jewelry only
   c. earrings and bracelets only

3. How long will this sale last?
   a. two hours
   b. three hours
   c. one hour

Jenny's New Car: Part One

Your friend is telling you a story about her sister Jenny's experience buying a car. Listen to the first part of the story.

___ on its last legs   ___ pay an arm and a leg   ___ call it quits

___ take advantage of   ___ a lemon   ___ in other words

___ pulling her leg   ___ believe it or not   ___ put something off

Questions

Answer the questions about your friend's story. Use the idiom given in parentheses in your answer. Be sure to change the idiom to fit the rest of the sentence if necessary.

1. Why did Jenny want to buy a new car?

   _____

   (on its last legs)

2. Why did Jenny decide to buy a used car?

   _____

   (pay an arm and a leg)

3. What did Jenny think when she heard the price of the car?

_____

(pull one's leg)

4. Why was the car so cheap?

_____

(call it quits)

Jenny's New Car: Part Two

Now listen as your friend tells you the rest of the story about Jenny's car.

____ on one's last legs   ____ pay an arm and a leg   ____ call it quits

____ take advantage of   ____ a lemon   ____ in other words

____ pulling one's leg   ____ believe it or not   ____ put something off

Questions

Answer the questions about your friend's story. Use the idiom given in parentheses in your answer. Be sure to change the idiom to fit the rest of the sentence if necessary.

1. What kind of car did Jenny probably buy?

_____

(a lemon)

2. Are Jenny's car repairs expensive? Explain your answer.

_____

(pay an arm and a leg)

3. What does Jenny's sister think about the car salesman?

_____

(take advantage of)

Holding Your Own...

Fill in each blank in the following conversation with one of the idioms listed on the following page. You will not use all of the idioms, and you should not use any idiom more than one time. Be sure to make any necessary changes in the idiom to agree with the rest of the sentence.

- on one's last legs
- take advantage of
- pulling one's leg
- pay an arm and a leg
- in other words
- believe it or not
- call it quits
- put something off
- a lemon

ANDY'S SCIENCE PROJECT

Andy is working on a science project for school. He's telling a friend about his progress.

ANDY: I've been having problems with my project and I'm almost ready to _____.

FRIEND: Don't give up yet. You should _____ the school's science laboratory. It's in Room 23. Have you seen it?

ANDY: Room 23! _____ that's where I've been working all day today. I worked with three different pieces of equipment and each one was _____.

FRIEND: Really? You're _____. I thought the school put all new equipment in that room last year.

ANDY: They were thinking about that, but then they found out how much it would cost. They said they didn't have the money to _____ for everything.

FRIEND: So, _____, they just kept all the old equipment and didn't buy anything new. . . .

ANDY: That's right. Now it's almost impossible to finish my experiment, so I'm going to think of a new one. Luckily, I have two weeks to work on this. I'm sure glad I didn't _____ doing the work before this!

WHAT WOULD YOU SAY?

Read each of the following situations. Then answer each question using one of the idioms below. You may need to use some idioms more than once, but try to use as many different idioms as possible. Make each answer a complete sentence. Be sure to change the idiom to fit the rest of the sentence if necessary.

- on one's last legs   • pay an arm and a leg   • call it quits
- take advantage of   • in other words   • put something off
- pulling one's leg   • believe it or not   • a lemon

1. Rick's dog is 18 years old and very sick. What might Rick say about his dog's condition?

    _____

    _____

2. Harry bought too much food for the party. He spent hundreds of dollars on food for only 20 people. He even spent over $200 on cakes and cookies. What can you say about how much Harry spent?

    _____

    _____

3. Your brother bought a very expensive video camera, but it doesn't take very good pictures. He brought it back to the store three times. Each time they said they fixed it, but he's still having problems with it. What might you say about his camera?

    _____

    _____

4. Daniel has been studying for a big test. It's 3:00 A.M. now and he's too tired to study anymore. What do you think Daniel should do now?

    _____

    _____

5. Fumiko wants to go to an expensive university, but she doesn't have enough money to go there. She just found out she won a scholarship to that school. What do you think she will do?

    _____

    _____

6. Bob's big report is due tomorrow, but he hasn't finished it yet. The boss gave him this assignment last week, and he started to work on it this morning. Why do you think Bob's report is not finished?

   _____

   _____

7. Today is January 3, 1991, and tomorrow is Anna's birthday. She was born in 1950. Write a sentence about Anna's age. If you think Anna looks young for her age, can you think of a different sentence to write about her?

   _____

   _____

8. Markus learned to play tennis about one month ago. Yesterday he played tennis with his friend Tom. Tom has been playing tennis for about a year. Write a surprising statement about how Markus played tennis yesterday.

   _____

   _____

9. Greg and Janice went out to dinner at an expensive restaurant yesterday. At the end of the dinner, Greg realized he had left his money and credit cards at home. Janice said she didn't have any money, but she really did. Why did Janice say that?

   _____

   _____

Wrapping It Up ....

Your teacher will give you a partner or put the class into groups. With your partner or group, choose one of the pictures on the next page. Read the information about the picture and follow the instructions about writing a story or conversation. Be prepared to share your work with the class.

The two people in the picture above are a boss and an office worker. The office worker is showing the boss that the desk is broken. They are talking about what to do with the desk and how to solve the problem. With your partner or group, write the conversation they are having or a short story about this situation. Be sure to use as many idioms from this unit as you can.

In the bottom picture on page 52, Anthony de la Torre and his son Nick are in their garage. They are trying to fix an old air conditioner that is broken. With your partner or group, write the conversation they are having or a short story about this situation. Be sure to use as many idioms from this unit as you can.

Talking It Over...

1. Have you ever bought anything that was a lemon? What did you do with it after you found out about its problems?

2. Do you own anything that's on its last legs? If so, describe it to the class and explain why it's in bad condition.

3. Have you ever called it quits when you thought you could not succeed or finish something? Exactly why did you give up?

4. Are you the type of person who puts things off? Is this a good or bad habit in your opinion?

LESSON 6
Review: Lessons 1-5

I. CROSSWORD PUZZLE #1

All of the idioms in the following crossword puzzle contain two words and are found in lessons 1–5 in this book.

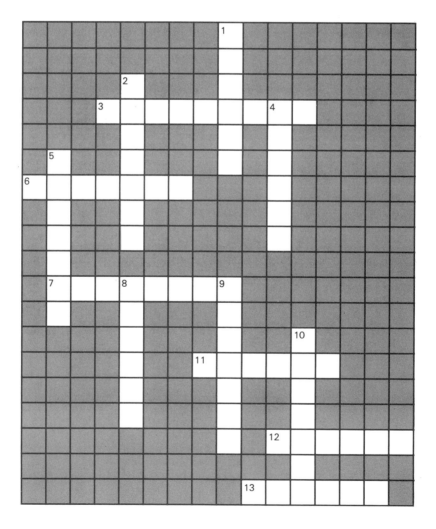

Across
3. immediately
6. have no money
7. before
11. submit
12. please
13. delay

Down
1. actually
2. get information
4. a bad product
5. want
8. visit
9. solve a problem
10. write information on a form

II. CROSSWORD PUZZLE #2

All of the idioms in the following crossword puzzle contain three or four words and are found in lessons 1–5 in this book.

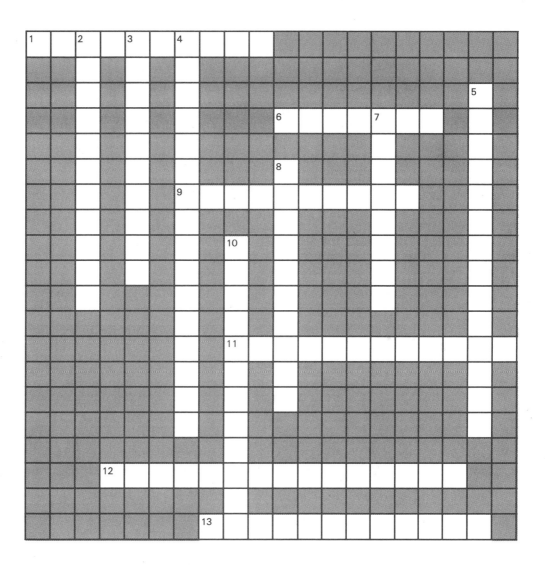

Across
1. start before the correct time
6. usually
9. responsible for
11. pity
12. use or benefit from
13. to say it in another way

Down
2. write down
3. go slowly
4. meal with a special price
5. look at/listen to carefully
7. current
8. give attention to
10. without warning

III. MATCHING

Match the idioms in the column on the left with their meanings in the column on the right. Put the letter of the meaning next to each number on the left. You will not use all of the meanings.

___ 1. believe it or not

___ 2. change one's mind

___ 3. make up one's mind

___ 4. on its last legs

___ 5. out of the question

___ 6. pay an arm and a leg

___ 7. take a raincheck

___ 8. up to you

a. your decision

b. impossible

c. spend a lot of money

d. ask for another invitation

e. have a new idea or opinion

f. win some money

g. decide

h. it's the truth

i. in bad condition

IV. MEANINGS

Next to each number below you will find several words or expressions. In each group there is one that has a different meaning from the others. Find the one that has the different meaning and put a circle around it.

Example:

little	(big)	small	tiny
1. stop	give up	begin	call it quits
2. contact	get in touch with	stay away from	communicate with
3. not have a leg to stand on	have a good reason	have a bad story	not have a good excuse
4. dislike	feel like	want to	in the mood for
5. pull someone's leg	play a joke	fool someone	make someone fall down
6. change someone's thinking	have a short talk with someone	convince	talk someone into something
7. I agree	I have the same opinion	that makes two of us	I have a different opinion
8. honestly	to tell you the truth	actually	unfortunately

9. say yes   say no   turn someone down   refuse

V. LISTENING PRACTICE

Listen to the questions for this exercise. Then write an answer to each question below. You must use one of the idioms given in parentheses in your answer. You may need to write two sentences (to explain the situation) for some answers. If possible, give more than one answer, using a different idiom each time.

1. (jump the gun/not have a leg to stand on/a lemon)

_____

_____

_____

_____

2. (on its last legs/turn someone down/take advantage of)

_____

_____

_____

_____

3. (all of a sudden/pay attention to/jump the gun)

_____

_____

_____

_____

4. (pay an arm and a leg/not have a leg to stand on/feel sorry for)

_____

_____

_____

_____

5. (fill out/that makes two of us/hand in)

_____

_____

_____

_____

VI. DICTATION AND ANSWER

• •

For this exercise you will do two things:
A. First, you will hear some questions. Write these questions in the spaces next to the numbers below.
B. After all of the questions have been written down, answer each one. Each of your answers must include one of the idioms listed below. Use a different idiom in each answer. (You will not use all of the idioms.)

• out of the question	• take care of	• take a raincheck
• in charge of	• in fact	• believe it or not
• in advance	• be broke	• take it easy
• to tell you the truth	• hand in	• clear up
• find out	• feel like	

1. _____

    _____?

    _____

    _____

2. _____

    _____?

    _____

    _____

3. _____

    _____?

    _____

    _____

4. _____
   _____?
   _____
   _____

5. _____
   _____?
   _____
   _____

VII. PROBLEM SOLVING—LANGUAGE LEARNING

Learning a new language can be a difficult experience. With your partner or group, discuss some of the problems or difficulties you have experienced while trying to learn a new language. Write these problems on the lines below, using as many of the idioms given as possible.

IDIOMS

- call it quits
- up-to-date
- feel like
- pay an arm and a leg
- pay attention to
- change one's mind
- in the mood
- clear up
- put off
- right away
- out of the question
- find out
- as a rule

PROBLEMS

_____
_____
_____
_____
_____
_____
_____
_____

_____

_____

_____

Now write down some solutions to these problems or suggestions on how to avoid these problems when learning a new language. Write your answers on the lines below, using as many of the idioms given as possible.

IDIOMS

• call it quits	• in other words	• get in touch with
• up-to-date	• up to someone	• take advantage of
• make a note of	• clear up	• find out
• take care of	• right away	• put off
• pay attention to	• as a rule	

SOLUTIONS

_____

_____

_____

_____

_____

_____

_____

_____

_____

_____

VIII. IDIOM GAME SHOW

Have you ever watched game shows on television? Have you ever wanted to be on one of these shows? Here's your chance to show how much you know about the idioms we have studied in the first five lessons.

This game can be played individually or in groups. Your teacher will decide how your class will play. If you play individually, each student should write the answers in the boxes below. If you play with a partner or in groups/teams, each pair or group should try to find the answers together and write them in the boxes below.

Look at the game board below. You will see numbers on the left. These numbers tell you how many points you will get for the correct answers. At the top of the board, you will see categories. These tell you what kind of idiom you will be asked about. (For example, in the column called "body parts," each question or answer will refer to a part of the body.)

Your teacher will give each person, pair, group, or team a chance to choose the category and number of points he/she/they wish to try. Then your teacher will tell you some information or ask a question about the idiom. You must try to give the correct answer. If you are correct, you will get the points. If you are not correct, you will get no points. You will take turns with the other people in your class to try to answer the questions, and the game will continue until all of the questions have been answered. The questions for 10 points are the easiest, and the questions for 50 points are the most difficult. GOOD LUCK!

	2 Words	3 Words	Body Parts	Begins with "In"	Begins with "T"
10 points					
20 points					
30 points					
40 points					
50 points					

IX. STORY GO 'ROUND

· ·

Look at the picture below. Your class is going to tell a story about what's happening in the picture. The teacher will ask one student to begin the story. This student must use one of the idioms we have reviewed in this lesson. Then the teacher will stop this student and ask another student to continue the story. This student must also use one of the idioms we have reviewed in this lesson. The teacher will continue to ask different students to continue the story. Each student must try to use a different idiom when s/he adds to the story.

LESSON 7

Getting Directions: Don't Get Lost

Getting Your Feet Wet ....

 Your teacher will give you a partner. Imagine this person is coming to your house (or apartment or dorm) after school today. Give her/him directions to your house from school. If necessary, you may draw a small map in the box below. If you draw a map, be sure to explain the directions as well as show them on the map.

 Today is Minoru's first day on campus at Hilltop College.

MINORU: Excuse me. I'm trying to find the bookstore, but I can't **find my way around** this campus. I have a map but I'm still confused.

STRANGER: You're looking for the bookstore? Hmm. That's pretty far away from here. In fact, it's on the other side of campus. Let me show you on the map. We're here, next to the Student Center. So you'll **start out** at these steps and walk straight ahead. **Keep your eye out for** the library. It'll be on the left. After you see the library, **keep on** walking in the same direction until you see the cafeteria.

MINORU: The cafeteria? Just a minute. Let me **make sure** I see that on the map. Oh, I see it. After I see the cafeteria, what should I do?

STRANGER: Just before the cafeteria, you'll **make a right** and you'll cross a
              small footbridge. The bookstore is on the other side of that
              bridge. You'll see it right away.

MINORU: Thanks so much for **taking the trouble to** help me. I hope I don't
              get lost again.

Getting the Picture ....

1. What building is Minoru looking for?
2. Where on campus are these two people talking?
3. How far away is the bookstore?
4. In which direction will Minoru start to walk?
5. What building should Minoru look for on the left?
6. In what direction will Minoru go at the cafeteria?
7. Where will Minoru see the bookstore?
8. Do you think Minoru will get lost again? Why or why not?

Figuring It Out ....

In each sentence in this exercise you will find one of the idioms from the
conversation. Look at how each idiom is used in the conversation and in the
sentence in this exercise. Then try to guess the meaning of each idiom. Write
the meaning on the line below each sentence.

1. When you go to a new city, it might be hard to **find your way around** without a map.

   *find one's way around*_____

2. We visited Europe last summer. We **started out** in Sweden and traveled all the way to Italy.

   start out _____

3. There are dangerous snakes on this mountain. **Keep your eye out for** them when you walk on this trail.

   keep one's eye out for _____

4. Octavio's mother told him to stop playing his electric guitar, but he didn't listen to her. He **kept on** playing it.

   keep on (doing something) _____

5. We must leave the house at 8:00 A.M., so please **make sure** you are ready at that time.

   make sure _____

6. At that corner you must **make a right** because no left turn is allowed there.

   make a right _____

7. Please don't **take the trouble to** get my coat for me. I can get it myself.

   *take the trouble to*_____   _____

8. Bob **got lost** trying to find the doctor's office. He had to stop and call for directions.

   get lost _____

Learning the Ins and Outs ....

Remember to change the possessive (one's) to agree with the subject in the following two idioms:

> **find one's way around**
> **keep one's eye out for**

Examples: They can't find **their** way around.
You can't find **your** way around.
I kept **my** eye out for the sign.
She kept **her** eye out for the sign.

keep on
Be sure to put an "ing" on the verb that follows this idiom.
Example: The referee blew his whistle, but the players kept on **kicking** the ball.

take the trouble to

This idiom is used when someone makes an effort to do something. Usually it shows that this was a difficult thing to do or that this person did not have to do it.

start out

This idiom means begin. When you want to say how you begin doing something, you can say start out **by doing something.** Be sure to put the "ing" on the verb that follows the "by" in this case.
Example: During our visit to New York, we **started out by visiting** the Empire State Building.

Catching On ....

CHOOSE THE MEANING

Choose the letter of the word or expression that has the same meaning as the italicized idiom in the sentence. In some cases only one word or expression has the same meaning as the idiom, while in other cases two words or expressions have the same meaning. Circle the letter(s) of your answers.

1. Veronique has lived in Paris all her life, so she *can find her way around* that city very well.
    a.   is able to move easily through
    b.   isn't able to move easily through
    c.   can travel through

2. Sam lives on this street. *Keep your eye out for* his house.
    a.   listen for
    b.   look for
    c.   watch for

3. At the stop sign, *make a right* and then you will see the movie theater.
    a.   go straight
    b.   turn right
    c.   turn correctly

4. The little boy walked away from his mother at the store, and then he *got lost*.
    a.   lost his money
    b.   lost his way
    c.   became lost

5. Mrs. Mendez is so thoughtful. Yesterday she *took the trouble to* help her neighbors, and then she invited them to dinner.
    a.   made no effort to
    b.   made a problem to
    c.   made an effort to

6. This morning we *started out* for the beach, but then it became cloudy and cold so we went back home.
   a. decided
   b. began
   c. waited

7. Please call me later. If I'm not home, *keep on* trying to telephone me.
   a. continue
   b. don't stop
   c. forget about

8. I think I can go with you to the concert. Let me look at my calendar to *make sure* I'm not busy that night.
   a. write down
   b. check
   c. be positive

LISTENING

After each number, you will hear two sentences, A and B. In each case one sentence will contain one of the idioms from this lesson. In some cases the two sentences will have the same meaning, and in other cases they will not. Listen carefully. Then circle the word "same" if you think the sentences have the same meaning, or "different" if you think they do not have the same meaning. You will be listening for the general meaning; the two sentences do not have to be **EXACTLY** the same.

1. SAME   DIFFERENT

2. SAME   DIFFERENT

3. SAME   DIFFERENT

4. SAME   DIFFERENT

5. SAME   DIFFERENT

6. SAME   DIFFERENT

7. SAME   DIFFERENT

8. SAME   DIFFERENT

Holding Your Own...

LATE FOR THE PARTY

Fill in each blank in the following conversations with one of the idioms listed below. You should use each idiom only one time. Be sure to make any necessary changes in the idiom to agree with the rest of the sentence.

- find one's way around
- make a right
- make sure
- start out
- take the trouble to
- keep on
- keep one's eye out for
- get lost

Frank and Jill have just arrived at their friend Tom's house for a party.

TOM: Hi Frank. Hi Jill. Thanks for coming tonight.

FRANK: We're glad to be here finally. We couldn't _____ your neighborhood very well.

TOM: Did you _____? I thought Debbie gave you directions last night.

JILL: She did, but we lost them. We didn't want to _____ get them again. We thought we could remember how to get here.

FRANK: We _____ fine, and then I guess we made a wrong turn somewhere.

JILL: I remembered to _____ the library on Bleeker Street, but when I forgot to _____ at Dove Street. We just _____ going down Bleeker.

TOM: Well, I'm sure glad you got here. Come in and meet everyone. And _____ you get something to eat and drink from the kitchen.

AT THE EMPLOYMENT AGENCY

Manuela has recently moved to a new city and is looking for a job. She has just arrived at an employment agency and is now talking to the employment counselor. On the following page you will find parts of their conversation. On each line you should complete the sentence or write a sentence to fit the conversation. Be sure to use the idiom in parentheses in each of your answers. Remember to change the idiom to fit the sentence if necessary.

1. COUNSELOR: I see on your application that you're new to this city. How do you like it here?

   MANUELA: So far I love it. It's such a big, exciting city. _____

   _____

   (get lost)

   COUNSELOR: That makes two of us! I've lived here for five years and _____

   _____

   (find one's way around)

2. MANUELA: I've never been to an employment agency before. How does this work?

   COUNSELOR: _____

   (start out)

   MANUELA: I see. Then after that you'll send me to some companies for an interview?

   COUNSELOR: Yes. And if you don't get the job, _____

   _____

   (keep on)

3. COUNSELOR: Here are the papers. Please fill them out immediately. _____

   _____

   (make sure)

   MANUELA: I have my resume with me. Would you like that too? Do I still need to fill out all these forms?

   COUNSELOR: Your resume will give me most of the information I need. Just complete the white form for now. _____

   _____ the yellow form.

   (take the trouble to)

4. COUNSELOR: Thanks for coming in today. I'm sure I'll be calling you soon for an interview.

   MANUELA: I hope so. Before I leave, could you tell me how to find the uptown subway station from here?

   COUNSELOR: Sure. When you leave this building, you'll be on Fifth Avenue.

   You want 54th Street, so _____
   (make a right)

   Then walk about two blocks and _____

   _____.

   (keep one's eye out for)

   The station will be on the next corner.

Wrapping It Up ....

Your teacher will assign you a partner. One of you will be **PARTNER A** and the other will be **PARTNER B**. If you are **PARTNER A**, read only the information under **PARTNER A** below. Then look at your map and follow the instructions given. If you are **PARTNER B**, read only the information under **PARTNER B** below. Then look at your map and follow the instructions given.

Partner A
• • • • • • • • • • •

Look at the map below. Some of the buildings and places have names, while others do not. Your partner has the same map with different buildings and places labeled. You and your partner are going to give each other directions to find certain places on the map.

You are at the post office and you want to go to the bank, but you don't know where the bank is. Tell your partner where you are and where you want to go, and s/he will give you directions. As your partner gives you the directions, draw your route (starting at the post office) on this map.

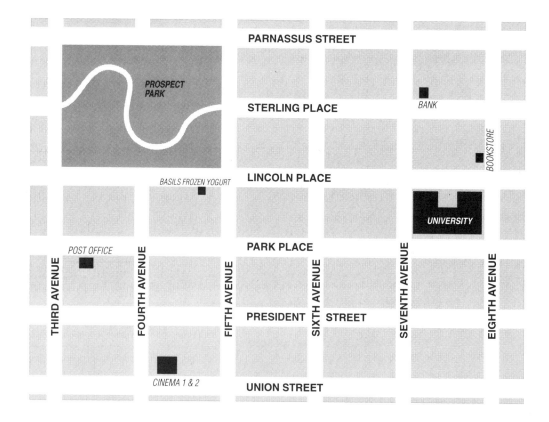

Partner B
••••••••••

Look at the map below. Some of the buildings and places have names, while others do not. Your partner has the same map with different buildings and places labeled. You and your partner are going to give each other directions to find certain places on the map.

You are at the park and you want to go to the subway station, but you don't know where the subway station is. Tell your partner where you are and where you want to go, and s/he will give you directions. As your partner gives you the directions, draw your route (starting at the park) on this map.

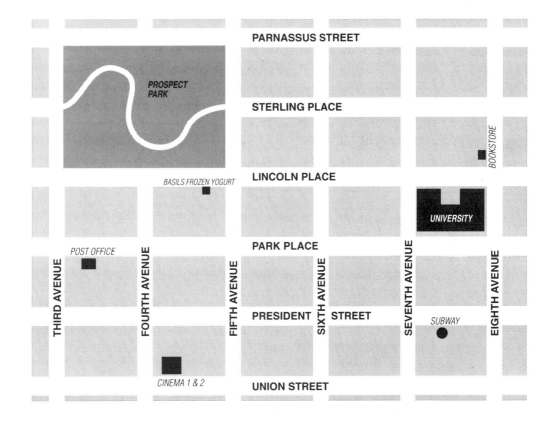

Talking It Over ....

1. Is it easy or difficult to find your way around the city you now live in? Explain your answer.
2. Have you ever traveled to a new city or country and gotten lost? Tell the class the story.
3. Read the following problems/situations. Imagine you are at each situation and you want to help. What could you take the trouble to do in each case?
   a. A car in front of you has just had an accident. The driver is not getting out of the car.
   b. You are in a busy store and a small child is crying. She seems lost and you don't see an adult with her.
   c. You are walking down the street and someone asks you where the nearest post office is.

LESSON 8
The Bus Tour: Showing You Around the City

Getting Your Feet Wet ....

1. Congratulations! You have just won a free trip. You can choose to go any-where in the world for one week. Where will you go? Why did you choose this place, and what do you want to see there? Discuss this with a partner and be prepared to tell the class about it.
2. Look at the photo below. What city do you think this is? Do you like to visit big cities? What is your favorite city and why?

You are taking a bus tour of a city you are visiting for the first time. Listen as the guide begins the tour.

Hello, everyone. Welcome to the Clover Line afternoon tour of downtown. My name is Robin, and in a few minutes we'll be starting our tour. Before we begin, I'd like to remind you to stay seated and keep your hands inside the bus **at all times.** Oh, **by the way,** this is our bus driver, Phil, and he'll be helping me **show you around.** If you have any questions along the way, please **feel free to** ask either me or Phil.

Our tour this afternoon will take about three hours, and during that time we're going to be **covering a lot of ground.** We will be making short stops at Old Town, Chinatown, and Broadway Plaza. That will give you a chance to **take some pictures** and **pick up** a few souvenirs. When we make these stops, you'll have only a few minutes to walk around. So please try to **keep up with** the group. We certainly don't want anyone to get lost on this tour!

Well, it's 12 o'clock; I guess it's time to **get going.** We want to thank you for choosing Clover Line today and hope you enjoy the tour. So now, sit back and relax, and let us **lead the way** for the next few hours.

Getting the Picture ....

1. Where is this tour going?
2. What does Robin remind the tourists about?
3. Who is Phil and what will he do?
4. What can the tourists do during the stops?
5. How much time will the tourists have during the stops?
6. What time does this tour start?

Figuring It Out ....

In each sentence in this exercise you will find one of the idioms in the tour information Robin gave above. You will also find a list of meanings below. Look at how each idiom is used in the information above and in the sentence in this exercise. Find the meaning that matches each idiom. Then try to think of another meaning or synonym for as many of these idioms as possible.

MEANINGS

• always	• travel over a large area	• while I think of it
• go the same speed as	• give a tour of	• get
• leave	• be the leader	• be comfortable to

1. During the short airplane flight, the passengers were told to keep their seat belts on **at all times.**

    another meaning _____

2. Good morning, Cindy. How are you today? Oh, **by the way,** did you finish that report for me yet?

    another meaning _____

3. Many of my friends and family come to San Diego to visit. I love to **show them around** the city, so they can see all the interesting places.

    another meaning _____

4. I'm leaving the office now. If you need to work on a computer, please **feel free to** use mine while I'm out.

    another meaning _____

5. I'm going to shop at that new department store tomorrow because they're having a grand opening sale. I hope I can **pick up** some good bargains.

    another meaning _____

6. Yesterday we **covered a lot of ground** and saw many things. I think I'll stay in the hotel and get some rest today.

    another meaning _____

7. We're late for the bus. If you **keep up with** me, maybe we can get to the bus stop quickly.

    another meaning _____

8. The show is going to start at 8:00 P.M. We need to **get going** soon if we want to get there on time.

    another meaning _____

9. You know so much about this zoo. You should **lead the way** and we'll follow you.

    another meaning _____

Learning the Ins and Outs ....

show someone around
Be sure to change **someone** to the person being shown around.

Examples: I showed **him** around.
He showed **me** around.
They showed **us** around.
We showed **Alice** around.

by the way
> This is an informal expression. Usually it is used to give additional or extra information in conversation. Do not use this expression in writing.

feel free to
> This expression is often used in informal situations. It means that the speaker wants you to be comfortable to do something by yourself. You do not have to ask permission to do something.

cover a lot of ground
> This expression can be used in different situations. It can be used when you are traveling and going to many places. It can also be used when you are getting a lot of new information or learning many new things.
> Examples: When we went to Italy, we saw many cities.
> **We covered a lot of ground** in one week.
> I have so much to study for my French class.
> Mr. Brunot **covered a lot of ground** in his lecture yesterday.

pick up something/pick something up
> This expression is informal when you use it to mean get or buy something.
> This idiom can be used in two ways by changing the position of the word **up** in the sentence.
> Examples: I **picked up** this souvenir on the tour.
> I **picked** this souvenir **up** on the tour.
> I **picked** it **up** on the tour.
> (This idiom works in the same way as the idioms in "Learning the Ins and Outs" in Lesson 1—see page 4.)

keep up with
> This idiom means to go the same speed as someone or something, or not to fall behind someone.
> Examples: I **kept up with** my brother during the hike.
> (This means I hiked as fast as my brother did/I did not fall behind.)
> You can also keep up with information.
> Examples: I **keep up with** the news by reading the newspaper every day.
> I'm dropping that math class. The teacher covers too many chapters each lesson.
> I can't **keep up with** the work.

Catching On...

FIND THE RESPONSE

Next to each number in the column on the left, you will find the beginning of a conversation. Next to each letter in the column on the right, you will find some responses. Find the response on the right that fits each sentence or question on the left. Choose the letter of the correct answer. Write the letter next to the number on the left. You will not use one response.

_____ 1. Can we walk around the bus while we're traveling?

_____ 2. By the way, where is your brother working now?

_____ 3. Thanks for coming to my party. Feel free to get some food in the dining room.

_____ 4. We'd like to see the dormitory; our son wants to live here.

_____ 5. I was absent last week. Will I be prepared for the test tomorrow?

_____ 6. Can you pick up a few things at the supermarket for me?

_____ 7. Can you walk more slowly? I can't keep up with you.

_____ 8. I think I'm lost. Do you have the map with you?

_____ 9. It's late and I really have to get going now.

a. One of our student assistants will be happy to show you around.

b. I'm not going there now, but I might go later tonight.

c. I don't know. We covered a lot of ground in class; you'll have to study hard.

d. Yes. I see where we are. I'll lead the way.

e. It was great to see you again. Next time don't leave so early!

f. He's retired right now. He might get a part-time job, though.

g. Thanks. Everything looks great and I'm hungry.

h. No, the driver says you must sit in your seats at all times.

i. Sorry, but I don't want to be late for school again.

j. Well, thanks for coming. It was great to see you again.

LISTENING

You are going to hear three short listening passages two times. You will do two things after you hear each passage:

1. In each part below you will see a list of the idioms from this lesson. Listen for any of these idioms in each passage. As you listen to each passage for the first time, put a check in the space provided next to each idiom you hear.

2. After you hear each passage the second time, answer the questions.

Postal Worker's Announcement

You are at a busy post office. Listen to the postal worker's announcement.

___ lead the way   ___ show someone around   ___ get going

___ by the way   ___ at all times   ___ pick up

___ feel free to   ___ cover a lot of ground   ___ keep up with

Questions

Answer the questions about the postal worker's announcement. Circle the letter of the correct answer.

1. What must the customers do at all times?
   a. They must always send an insured package.
   b. They must wait in one line.
   c. They must complete an insurance form to pick up a package.

2. What should the customers feel free to do if they have a package?
   a. walk up to a clerk for help
   b. send an insured package without an insurance form
   c. complete an insurance form while waiting in line

3. How can a customer pick up a package?
   a. S/he must wait in one line.
   b. S/he must fill out an insurance form.
   c. S/he must bring a yellow slip to the counter.

At the Museum

Mrs. O'Leary's class is visiting a museum. Listen to her as she talks to her class.

___ lead the way   ___ show someone around   ___ get going

___ by the way   ___ at all times   ___ pick up

___ feel free to   ___ cover a lot of ground   ___ keep up with

Questions

Answer the questions about what Mrs. O'Leary told her class. Use the idiom given in parentheses in your answer. Be sure to change the idiom to fit the rest of the sentence if necessary.

1. Will these students see much of the museum or only a little bit of it?

    _____

    (cover a lot of ground)

2. Can the students visit each area by themselves? Why or why not?

    _____

    (keep up with/at all times)

3. Who will take the group up to the third floor now?

    _____

    (lead the way)

At the Business Meeting

Kathy Mendoza is going to give a report at a business meeting. Listen to how she begins.

___ lead the way   ___ show someone around   ___ get going

___ by the way   ___ at all times   ___ pick up

___ feel free to   ___ cover a lot of ground   ___ keep up with

Answer the questions about Kathy's talk. Circle the letter of the correct answer.

1. What is Kathy going to cover a lot of ground about in her talk?
    a. Frank Sforza's work on this project
    b. a new business park
    c. several projects she is working on

2. What does Kathy want the people at the meeting to feel free to do?
    a. ask her questions
    b. see the office with her or Frank
    c. ask Frank questions after the talk only

3. What will help everyone keep up with Kathy while she is talking?
    a. She will give each person a tour of the office now.
    b. She will stop and ask them questions during her talk.
    c. She has prepared some papers for them to look at.

4. Why do Kathy and Frank want to show people around the office?
    a. to show them pictures of the new business park
    b. to show them their offices only
    c. to show them some other projects

Holding Your Own..

Fill in each blank in the following conversation with one of the idioms listed below. You will not use all of the idioms, and you should not use any idiom more than one time. In some cases more than one answer may be correct.

HIKING UP THE MOUNTAIN

Claudia and Patrick are hiking in the mountains this afternoon. Claudia has done this hike before, and she knows the area well. This is Patrick's first time on this mountain.

• lead the way	• show someone around	• get going
• by the way	• at all times	• pick up
• feel free to	• cover a lot of ground	• keep up with

PATRICK: Well, Claudia, since you know this area pretty well, you should _____.

CLAUDIA: Okay. This is a beautiful park. How far do you want to go? There's so much to see here. We can _____ if you want to.

PATRICK: I don't know. I haven't gone hiking in a while. I hope I can _____ you. Maybe we should take it easy today.

CLAUDIA: Okay. We can take the short trail. It doesn't go to the top of the mountain, but we'll see some lakes and streams. If you get too tired, _____ tell me to stop and rest.

PATRICK: Thanks. Oh, _____, where can I get some drinking water? My water bottle is empty.

CLAUDIA: There's a drinking fountain over there, next to the park office. In fact, while you're there, you can _____ a map of the park.

PATRICK: Good idea. I'll be back in a few minutes and then we can _____.

WHAT'S THE QUESTION?

Complete each of the following conversations by making a question that will fit the answer given. Be sure to use the idiom given in parentheses in your question and to change it to agree with the rest of the sentence if necessary.

1. A: _____?

   (at all times)

   B: Yes, that's the only pencil that the machine can read to score the test.

2. A: _____?

   (by the way)

   B: No, I haven't seen her in a long time. Maybe we should get in touch with her.

3. A: _____?

   (show someone around)

   B: No thanks. We're waiting for a friend. He's going to take us to the museum.

4. A: _____?

    (feel free to)

    B: Yes, of course. When you're ready to try on some clothes, I'll take you to the dressing room.

5. A: _____?

    (cover a lot of ground)

    B: Yes. I hope you're wearing comfortable shoes for this trip.

6. A: _____?

    (pick up)

    B: No, nothing is for sale at this museum. But we can look for a gift shop later.

7. A: _____?

    (keep up with)

    B: You should be able to. We're only going to walk around the lake.

8. A: _____?

    (get going)

    B: It's too early now. We can wait another half an hour.

9. A: _____?

    (lead the way)

    B: You probably should. I think you know this part of the city better than the rest of us.

Wrapping It Up ....

Read each of the following situations. Then write an answer to each question. Use one of the idioms we studied in this lesson in each of your answers. Each answer should be a complete sentence. Be sure to use each idiom at least one time. You may give more than one answer for each one if you can.

1. You and a friend are working on a report for school. You are at the library right now. Your friend asks you how long you think you will be working in the library. What is a possible answer to your friend's question?

   _____

   _____

2. Today is your first day on a new job. You need to find the copy machine and the mail room. Another worker has offered to help you. What might this worker say to offer help? As this worker is taking you to one of these places, what might you say?

   _____

   _____

3. The Simon family has just arrived in London for a vacation. They are in their hotel room, getting ready to go out and see the city. Mrs. Simon is telling everyone where they are going and what they will do this afternoon. Mr. Simon is giving everyone some advice about how to travel together. Their teenage daughter is telling them what she wants to do. What is Mrs. Simon saying? What is Mr. Simon saying? What is their daughter saying? (You should try to give more than one answer for each person.)

   Mrs. Simon: _____

   _____

   _____

   Mr. Simon: _____

   _____

   _____

   Daughter: _____

   _____

   _____

4. Paula and Enrique are old friends. They haven't seen each other for a long time, but they just met each other in the street. They are both late for work, so they don't have much

time to talk. What do you think they are saying as they are ending their conversation?

Paula: _____

_____

Enrique: _____

_____

5. You are at a supermarket, and there is a lady giving out samples of a new kind of fruit juice. She is trying to get people to taste this drink and then buy it. What do you think she is saying to the shoppers?

_____

_____

6. Tonight Rosa and Manuel are going out to dinner, and then they will see a movie. It's 5:45 P.M. now, and they have dinner reservations for 6:00 P.M. at the restaurant. Rosa is telling Manuel about the time. What will she say?

_____

_____

7. You are visiting Chicago for the first time, and you have just arrived at the airport. You are taking a taxi to your hotel. The taxi driver is very friendly, and you have just told him this is your first visit to this city. What might the taxi driver be saying to you?

_____

_____

Talking It Over...

1. Imagine you must give some advice to international travelers (people going to other countries). What would you tell them to be sure to do at all times?
2. When you travel, do you cover a lot of ground, or do you prefer to see one or two places? Explain your answer.
3. What place do you know best? (It can be a city, town, state, country, etc.) Have you ever shown a visitor around this place? If so, where did you take this person? If not, what two or three places would you take a visitor to see if you wanted to show him/her around?

LESSON 9

Sports: Keep Your Eye on These Events

Getting Your Feet Wet ....

1. What sports do you enjoy playing? How old were you when you began to play sports? Are children encouraged to play sports in your country?
2. What are the most popular sports in your native country? Do people in your country take sports or games very seriously? (Are sports/games serious events in your country?) Do teams in your country participate in international competitions? What competitions have they won?

3. Do people often go to stadiums or other places to watch sporting events in your country? Are many sporting events on the radio or television in your country?
4. Which sports are most popular in the United States? Do you know how to play any of these sports? Are they played in your country?
5. Is competition important in your country? Do you find much competition in school or at work?

It's Sunday afternoon and Rosanna wants to watch some television. She is trying to find something interesting to watch. Right now there are some sports events on. Listen as she changes from one station to another.

. . . As the runners come to the final lap of the race, it's Susan Smith in first place, Lisa Hernandez in second place, and Paula McCoy in third. Susan has been **way ahead of** all the others this whole race. Here she comes now; she has just crossed the finish line and **won by a mile. Keep your eye on** Susan; she's going to be a top runner this year. And here come Lisa and Paula fighting for second place. **At first,** it looked like Lisa was going to take second place easily, but now it looks like Paula is pulling ahead. Yes, Paula McCoy has just finished second. What an exciting race!

     CLICK

. . . So football fans, here we are in the last quarter of the second game of the season, and the Bullets are **in hot water** again. With only 12 seconds left in the game, it doesn't look like a touchdown is possible. The ball has been **back and forth** between both teams several times in the last 10 minutes, and now it's a **race against time.** Wait a minute. Jeffers has just caught the ball and is running down the field. He's at the 40 yard line, the 30, the 20. **I can't believe my eyes,** ladies and gentlemen. It's a touchdown, and the Bullets move ahead 14-10 with only one second left to play. Those Bullets really **gave it their best shot.**

Getting the Picture ....

1. Who wins the race in the first program Rosanna listens to?
2. Is it a difficult race for her or does she win it easily? How do you know?
3. Who comes in second place in this race? Was this easy or difficult for her?
4. Which team is losing when Rosanna first listens to the football game?
5. What happens at the end of the game?
6. How does the announcer feel at the end of the game?

Figuring It Out ....

In each sentence in this exercise you will find one of the idioms from the conversation. Look at how each idiom is used in the conversation and in the sentence in this exercise. Then try to guess the meaning of each idiom. Write the meaning on the line below each sentence.

1. John started to hike up this mountain an hour ago, so he's **way ahead of** me. I can't see him at all.

   way ahead of _____

2. No other car can go as fast as John's. In every race his car **wins by a mile.**

   win by a mile _____

3. When you're at the circus, **keep your eye on** the tall clown; he's the funniest.

   keep one's eye on someone _____

4. **At first,** the little girl was afraid of the water. Then, she jumped into the ocean and began to play in the waves.

   at first _____

5. Steve forgot to bring home some important papers from school. He's going to be **in hot water** with his parents.

   in hot water _____

6. In tennis, the players must hit the ball **back and forth** over the net and within the lines of the court.

   back and forth _____

7. It was a **race against time** for the ambulance to get to the car accident in time to save the man's life.

   race against time _____

8. **I can't believe my eyes;** I just saw a horse running down Main Street in between all the cars.

   can't believe one's eyes _____

9. A: Do you remember geometry? I'm having trouble with this homework.

   B: I studied it a long time ago, so I don't remember too much. I'll **give it my best shot,** though.

   give it one's best shot _____

Learning the Ins and Outs ....

Remember to change the possessive (one's) to agree with the subject in the following idioms:

> **keep one's eye on someone/something**
> **can't believe one's eyes**
> **give it one's best shot**

Examples: **I** kept **my** eye on the ball.
She can't believe **her** eyes.
You should give it **your** best shot.

ahead of/way ahead of
The expression **ahead of** means something is in front of something or someone. If you want to say something is very far in front, you can add the word **way** to this expression.

keep one's eye on something/someone
This idiom can be used in different ways.
1. Sometimes this expression means to watch or look at something or someone.
Examples: Kenny **kept his eye on the ball** and hit a home run.
The police officer **kept her eye on the boy** in the parking lot.
2. Sometimes this expression means to watch something (or someone) in order to take care of it.
Examples: Please **keep your eye on my money** while I go into the next room.
I have to go to the store for a few things. Could you **keep an eye on my children** for a few minutes?

can't believe one's eyes
This idiom can be used for different times.
Examples: Yesterday, **I couldn't believe my eyes** when I saw you.
I **can't believe my eyes**. I see Jennifer in the hall.
You **won't*** believe your eyes** when you see his new car.
(*Be sure to change the **can't** to **won't** for the future tense.)

race against time
This idiom can be used in two ways:
Examples: It was **a race against time** for the ambulance to
get to the accident.
The ambulance **raced against time** to get to
the accident.

Catching On ....

MATCHING

Match the idioms on the left with their meanings on the right. Put the letter of
the correct meaning in the space next to the number. You will not use all of the
meanings from the column on the right.

___ 1.   way ahead of

___ 2.   win by a mile

___ 3.   keep one's eye on something

___ 4.   at first

___ 5.   in hot water

___ 6.   back and forth

___ 7.   race against time

___ 8.   can't believe one's eyes

___ 9.   give it one's best shot

a.   very surprised at what one sees

b.   have a problem/in trouble

c.   something that must be finished by a certain time or deadline

d.   first one way, then the other

e.   watch/take care of

f.   try one's best

g.   in the beginning/initially

h.   stop quickly

i.   take first place easily

j.   far in front

LISTENING

Listen to the statements. Then look at the choices next to each number to find
an answer that makes sense with the statements. In some cases only one answer may be correct. In other cases two choices may be correct. Circle the let-
ter(s) of the correct answer(s).

Part A

1.   a.   Bill didn't finish the test.
b.   Bill finished after everyone else.
c.   Bill finished long before everyone else.

2. a. I think I'm a very fast runner.
   b. I usually beat you when I race you.
   c. I'll race you for one mile to the car.

3. a. You should watch the soup while it's cooking.
   b. You should cook the soup to a boil.
   c. You should make some pie and some soup.

4. a. I really don't think that's a famous opera singer.
   b. I'm very surprised because I think I see a famous opera singer.
   c. I see something unbelievable; it's a famous opera singer.

5. a. Jorge had a 6 o'clock deadline to be at the store.
   b. Jorge had to run to the store late at night.
   c. Jorge had to rush to get to the store before it closed.

Part B

1. a. At first, I'll order my new glasses.
   b. At first, I'll see the eye doctor.
   c. At first, I'll go on a date with Roger.

2. a. Gina is probably in hot water.
   b. Gregory is probably in hot water.
   c. Gregory had a problem with the hot water.

3. a. Jack keeps going back and forth between his old job and his new one.
   b. Jack likes to drive back and forth between Los Angeles and Riverside.
   c. Jack probably does a lot of back and forth driving every day.

4. a. He'll probably give the math problem his best shot.
   b. He thinks the math is easy, so he'll give it his best shot.
   c. He doesn't have to give it his best shot because he already knows the answer.

Holding Your Own..

On the following page you will find two short news articles with blank spaces. Fill in each of the blanks with one of the idioms below. You will use all of the idioms at least one time; you will also need to use some idioms more than one time. Be sure to make any changes in the idioms to agree with the rest of the sentence.

- (way) ahead of
- at first
- race against time
- win by a mile
- in hot water
- can't believe one's eyes
- keep one's eye on something
- back and forth
- give it one's best shot

Below is an article from the *Hoover Speedway News* about a car race. Be sure to add an idiom to the headline as well as the other blanks in the story.

ANDY COUGAR _____

Last night, Andy Cougar became the new champion of the Hoover Classic Car Race when he beat all the other drivers to the finish line by more than 12 seconds. _____, Joanne Beselco pulled out _____ everyone and Andy was only in third place. Then Andy came out in front, and for the last two laps he was _____ all the others. The crowd loved it; they _____.

After the race, Andy said, "I knew I could do it. I just _____."

Below is an article from Newtown High School's school newspaper about the school's math team.

NEWTOWN'S MATH TEAM WINS AGAIN

Last Tuesday night, Newtown's math team again took first place in the All-City Math Bowl. The three-member team won the contest in an exciting _____ _____ during the last minutes of the competition. Newtown's main competitor was Patrick Henry High, and the lead went _____ between the two teams for most of the night. Just before the final question, Newtown lost 2 points for an incorrect answer, and it looked like the team might be _____. But then, junior Rachel Bright correctly answered the final 20-point question to bring Newtown to victory. As a junior, Rachel will be able to join the team again next year, so _____ her. Other members of the team were Randy Sanchez and Ryan Karp. Congratulations to all the members of the team for again putting Newtown _____ all the other schools in the city.

ALL-CITY SCIENCE FIELD DAY

Yesterday an eight-hour science field day took place, with many different schools in the competition. You were able to attend this event until 12:00 noon, but your friend was not able to attend at all. Your friend wants to know what happened, so s/he is asking you questions about it. In this activity you will write the answers to your friend's questions.

Below you will find a chart with the results of the contests in the morning for four of the schools in the competition. Use this information to help you fill in some of the answers about this field day below. For some of your answers, you may not need the chart. Be sure to use the idioms given in parentheses in each answer you write. Make any changes that might be necessary to make the idioms fit the sentence.

School	9:00 A.M.	10:00 A.M.	11:00 A.M.	12:00 Noon
Encanto	40	80	100	130
Southridge	3	20	35	75
Willows	20	40	65	75
Mentor	5	15	40	45

1. When you left at 12:00 noon, how was the team from Mentor doing?

_____

(in hot water)

2. What did the students from Mentor say when you left at 12 o'clock?

_____

(give it one's best shot)

3. How was the team from Encanto doing at 12:00 noon?

_____

(way ahead of)

4. Which team did the best at the 10:00 A.M. event?

_____

(win by a mile)

5. Which team surprised you the most?

_____

(at first)

6. Which team do you think will finish in second place?

_____

(keep one's eye on)

7. Was the same team in last place all morning?

_____

(back and forth)

8. What happened to the Southridge team at the 9:00 A.M. event? Did they finish in time?

_____

(race against time)

9. Someone said the Encanto team finished the 11:00 A.M. event in 10 minutes. Is that true?

_____

(can't believe one's eyes)

Wrapping It Up...

Your teacher will assign you a partner or group for this activity.

1. Look at the illustration on the next page of a man and a woman talking to a police officer. These two people have just seen two men rob their neighbor's house, using a large truck. The family that lives in the house is not home today. The robbers used the truck so that people would think they were movers. (They didn't want anyone to know what they were really doing.) However, this man and woman finally realized the truth. They called the police. They tried to follow the truck when it left the house, but they couldn't because of traffic.

2. The two people talking to the police officer are telling her what they saw. The man is talking about how the robbers took many things out of the house and put them into the truck. The woman is talking about what happened when they tried to follow the robbers. They are both talking about what they did and how they feel about the situation.

3. With your partner(s), write the conversation you think is taking place between the police officer and these two people. You will need to write some of the police officer's questions as well as the answers from the man and woman. Use as many idioms from this lesson in your conversation as you can.

   You might want to think about the following when you write this conversation:

   • what the man and woman did while the robbers took things out of the house
   • why the man and woman waited to call the police
   • what the man and woman thought when they realized the truth
   • what happened when they tried to follow the truck
   • what they think about the robbers
   • what the police officer thinks about how the man and woman acted

Talking It Over..

1. Have you ever been in hot water in school, on your job, or at home? Describe the situation.
2. Describe a situation that you think would be difficult for you, but possible if you gave it your best shot.
3. At first, how did you feel when you were learning English? At first, how did you feel when you came to the United States?

LESSON 10

The Wedding: No Cutting Corners for This One

Getting Your Feet Wet..................................

1. Your teacher will assign you a partner or group. Tell your partner(s) about marriage/wedding customs in your country. Try to answer some of the following questions in your discussion.
    -   Do the man and woman usually decide to become engaged by themselves? Do they usually get permission from their parents first?
    -   Do people often have long engagements before they get married?
    -   What kind of wedding is most typical? Do people go to a church, temple, shrine, or other religious place for the ceremony? What do the bride and groom wear?

- Does a party or celebration follow the ceremony? Describe it.
- Who pays for the wedding? What kinds of presents are given to the couple getting married?

2. Look at the photo on page 96. Where are these people and what are they doing?

Janet and her husband have just returned home from a wedding. Janet is talking to the babysitter.

BABYSITTER:	How was the wedding?
JANET:	It was just beautiful. The ceremony started almost an hour late, though. I don't know why.
BABYSITTER:	**No wonder** you came home so late. Maybe the bride or groom **got cold feet.**
JANET:	I don't think so. Those two **get along** so well, and they've been planning this wedding for a long time. This is one marriage that I think will be **for good.**
BABYSITTER:	What about the reception? You had dinner at the Grand Hotel, didn't you?
JANET:	It was fantastic! They certainly didn't **cut corners** for this party. They had so much delicious food; I couldn't believe my eyes when I saw the buffet table. Every time I thought they might **run out of** food, another big dish was brought out. Her parents must be pretty **well-off** to make such a big, expensive affair.
BABYSITTER:	I'm glad to hear you had such a good time. Do you think you'll need me to babysit again next weekend?
JANET:	I'm not sure. We don't have any plans right now. I think we'll **play it by ear.**
BABYSITTER:	Okay. Just **let me know** if you need me.

Getting the Picture.....................................

1. Why does Janet think the ceremony started late? What does the babysitter think?
2. What kind of marriage does Janet think this will be? Why does she have this opinion?
3. Where was the reception for this wedding? What kind of reception was it?
4. What does Janet think about the bride's parents? Why?
5. Will Janet need the babysitter again next weekend?
6. Is the babysitter available to be there next weekend? How do you know?

Figuring It Out..

In each sentence below you will find one of the idioms in the conversation about the wedding. You will also find a list of meanings below. Look at how each idiom is used in the information given and in the sentence in this exercise. Find the meaning that matches each idiom. Then try to think of another meaning or synonym for as many of these idioms as possible.

MEANINGS

- it's not surprising
- tell someone
- reduce spending
- wealthy
- permanently
- become nervous
- make decisions as one goes along
- live or work well together
- use up all of something

1. Bernard wanted to ask his boss for a raise, but he **got cold feet** and decided to forget about it.

    another meaning _____

2. Jean's parents are **well-off.** They own two homes, three cars, and a boat.

    another meaning _____

3. You're looking at page 38, and we're working on page 35. **No wonder** you don't understand what we're doing.

    another meaning _____

4. When Gerry travels, he doesn't like to make plans. He just likes to go to a new city and **play it by ear** when he gets there.

    another meaning _____

5. Mr. Ritter is making reservations for a special dinner tonight. If you want to go, please **let him know** as soon as possible.

    another meaning _____

6. Alexander just lost his job, and his wife doesn't make much money. They will have to **cut corners** until they find good jobs.

    another meaning _____

7. Betty and Susana have many arguments. They usually don't **get along** with each other.

    another meaning _____

8. Steven decided he doesn't want to study karate anymore. He has quit karate **for good.**

    another meaning _____

9. Barbara forgot to put gas in the car yesterday. Then she **ran out of** gas while she was driving on the highway last night.

    another meaning _____

Learning the Ins and Outs ....

> **let someone know**
> This idiom means to contact someone about something or tell someone something. Remember to change the "someone" to the person you are telling, using either a pronoun or a noun.
> Examples: Please let **me** know as soon as possible.
>   Please let **Bob** know as soon as possible.

> **get along/get along (with someone)**
> This idiom can be used by itself or it may be followed by the preposition **with.**
> Examples: They **get along** very well.
>   He **gets along with** his brother very well.

Catching On ....

USING THE IDIOMS

Complete each statement or conversation by choosing from the **a, b, c** choices. In some cases only one choice is correct. In other cases two choices may be correct.

1. Sally's children don't get along very well with Maria's children. Sally
    a.   will probably invite Maria's children to her son's birthday party.
    b.   will probably not invite Maria's children to her son's birthday party.
    c.   will probably never speak to Maria again.

2. Joseph has an extra ticket to a concert tonight, so he invited Sylvie to go with him. Sylvie wasn't sure if she could go, so she said she would
    a.   let Joseph know later.
    b.   play it by ear.
    c.   get cold feet.

3. BOSS: I haven't seen James Malone. Where has he been the last two days?

    WORKER: He's sick. He'll probably be out for a few more days.

    BOSS: Oh. I didn't know that.

    a. No wonder he's been coming to work.
    b. That means he'll probably be out for good.
    c. No wonder he hasn't been here.

4. Fernando has decided to leave Smalltown and move to Chicago. He never wants to live in Smalltown again. He
    a. plans to leave Smalltown for good.
    b. will play it by ear about returning to Smalltown.
    c. has cold feet about leaving Smalltown.

5. Shannon decided to do a tap dance for her school talent show, but now she has cold feet. Shannon
    a. is very relaxed about dancing in the talent show.
    b. is nervous about dancing in the talent show.
    c. has a problem with her feet, so she can't dance.

6. That new restaurant has not been having very good business lately. If business continues this way, the owner
    a. will probably open another restaurant and become well-off.
    b. will probably have to cut corners and have fewer waitresses.
    c. may run out of money and close the restaurant.

7. Debbie wanted to bake a cake, but she found she had run out of eggs. Debbie could
    a. go to a neighbor and ask for some eggs.
    b. bake the cake immediately because she had enough eggs.
    c. wait to bake the cake until after she went to the supermarket.

8. Paul's sister is much more well-off than he is. Paul's sister
    a. is in better health than Paul is.
    b. has a much better education than Paul has.
    c. has more money than Paul has.

9. Today's weather reports say there may be a storm on Saturday. Richard and Pat want to go camping next weekend, but they will probably play it by ear. Richard and Pat
    a. will definitely go camping in the mountains next weekend.
    b. might go to the mountains if the weather is not bad.
    c. will wait to make their plans because of the possibility of bad weather.

LISTENING

You are going to hear several people leaving telephone messages on answering machines. Follow the directions for each of the following two parts.

Part A

Listen to each message in this part. Then choose the a, b, or c answer that best fits for each one. Circle the letter of your answer.

1. a. Amy's mom will let her know about the movie.
    b. Amy should let her mom know about the movie.
    c. The theater will let Amy's mom know about the movie.

2. a. Marcia plans to live alone for good.
    b. Bret plans to stay away from Marcia for good.
    c. Marcia and Bret plan to stay married for good.

3. a. George wants to go to the concert, but Amy wants to play it by ear.
    b. George wants to play it by ear for Saturday night.
    c. George wants to go to the concert and then listen to some music.

4. a. Mr. Bixby will cut corners and give Amy everything she wants for the party.
    b. Amy will not cut corners because she wants to spend more than $500.
    c. Amy will probably have to cut corners in order to make this party.

5. a. Bret and Marcia haven't been getting along very well lately.
    b. Bret and Marcia have been getting along very well lately.
    c. Bret likes Amy because he gets along so well with her.

Part B

The messages in this part are for your roommate and not for you. After you hear each one, write a message to your roommate in the box provided. Each message you hear in this part will contain one of the idioms. The message you write should **not** contain the idiom; you should write the message **in your own words.** Your message can be more than one sentence if necessary.

MESSAGES—TUESDAY

1. Mindy called. She _____

_____

_____

2. Peter called. He _____

_____

_____

---

3. Barbara called. She _____

_____

_____

4. Eugene called. He _____

_____

_____

Holding Your Own ·····································

THE INTERVIEW

The San Carlos Drama Club performed a play last weekend. Reporter Ricardo Lopez is writing an article for the local newspaper about the performance. He is interviewing some of the actors and the director of the production. Below you will find parts of his interviews.

Fill in each of the blank spaces of the interview with one of the idioms below. Be sure to change the idiom to fit the sentence if necessary. You should use each idiom only one time.

- for good
- well-off
- cut corners

- run out of
- let someone know
- get along

- get cold feet
- play it by ear
- no wonder

First, Ricardo talks with one of the actors.

RICARDO: I heard this is your first acting experience. How did you feel up on stage?

ACTOR: Well, just before I went out there, I started to _____. But as soon as I got onto the stage, I was fine.

RICARDO: You did a great job. I'm sure the audience never knew you were nervous. What was the best part of this production?

ACTOR: Oh, it was definitely working with these people. We all _____ so well. It was really a lot of fun.

RICARDO: Do you think you'll continue to perform with this drama club?

ACTOR: That's a good question. I'm not sure about that. You know, we don't get much money from such a small, local production. And I'm not _____ enough to do all this hard work for so little pay. Of course, it was so much fun. I think I'll just have to _____ and see how I feel later.

RICARDO: I see. Thanks for talking with me today.

Next, Ricardo talks to the director.

RICARDO: Congratulations on your success! It was an excellent performance.

DIRECTOR: Thank you. Yes, everyone worked very hard on this play. They should all be proud of their work, especially since we had so many problems.

RICARDO: I heard about the problem with money.

DIRECTOR: Problem? It was terrible! We had to _____ for everything. First, we had to ask the actors to make their own costumes, and then we _____ some of the makeup we needed for tonight's performance. I can't work like this. I'm leaving this drama club _____.

RICARDO: It's _____ you feel that way. Do you have any plans to do something else?

DIRECTOR: Actually, yes. I'm going to start my own production company. I've already found some people to work with me.

RICARDO: That sounds great. I'll be keeping an eye out for your next production. Here's my card. Be sure to _____ when and where your group is performing. I'll be there.

WEDDING PLANS

Nancy is getting married in several months, and she is planning her wedding. There are several people who are working with her to help make the day successful. Some of these people are:

- bridal shop salespeople/dressmakers (for dresses or gowns)
- wedding planners (people who earn money by organizing the wedding)
- caterers (people who make and serve the food for the party)

Below you will find some short, incomplete conversations between Nancy and these people. You must complete these conversations by writing a question or response that fits. You must use the idiom given in parentheses in your sentence.

At the Bridal Shop

1. SALESLADY: How much did you want to spend on your dress? You can rent a dress if it's too expensive to buy one.

   NANCY: No. _____

   _____
   (for good)

2. NANCY: This dress is so expensive. Who can afford to buy a dress like this?

   SALESLADY: _____

   _____
   (well-off)

3. SALESLADY: Isn't this a beautiful dress? It's made of the finest silk and has expensive pearls on it. Of course, it costs $10,000.

   NANCY: _____

   _____
   (no wonder)

4. SALESLADY: This dress looks just lovely on you. How does it feel to be wearing it?

   NANCY: _____

   _____
   (get cold feet)

The Wedding Planner

1. PLANNER: How do you want to arrange the seating for your family and the groom's family? Should we put them all at the same table?

   NANCY: _____

   _____

   (get along)

2. PLANNER: Do you prefer to have the champagne toast before, during, or after the dinner?

   NANCY: _____

   _____

   (play it by ear)

The Caterer

1. NANCY: We really didn't plan on spending this much money on the food. _____

   _____?

   (cut corners)

   CATERER: Well, we could serve only chicken and not have any seafood.

2. NANCY: _____

   _____?

   (let someone know)

   CATERER: Sure. But I need to have your final decision at least three weeks before the wedding.

3. NANCY: Do you think one large wedding cake will be enough for 200 people?

   CATERER: _____

   (run out of)

Wrapping It Up ....

Your teacher will assign you a partner or a group. With your partner(s), look at the illustration on page 106 and discuss what you see. Then, tell a short story about each person in the picture, using as many idioms from this lesson as possible. Be prepared to share your stories with the rest of the class. Lines have been provided, so that you can write each story down if you want to.

STORIES

the person at the bus stop

_____

_____

_____

_____

_____

_____

the person talking on the telephone

----

the people at the dentist's office

----

the people in front of the restaurant

----

the wealthy woman

Talking It Over ··

1. Have you ever gotten cold feet before you had to do something? What was the situation? Tell the class about your experience.
2. How many brothers and sisters do you have? Sometimes brothers and sisters don't get along with each other. How do you get along with your siblings?
3. Some people like to have an exact schedule for their activities. Others prefer to play it by ear in some situations. What do you prefer? In what situations are you comfortable playing it by ear?

LESSON 11
At the Airport: A Close Call

Getting Your Feet Wet ....

1. How often do you travel? When you do travel, is it usually for a vacation or for business? What kind of transportation do you prefer?
2. Is there a good public transportation system in your native city? How do most people get around that city? What kind of transportation is most popular in your native city or country?
3. What do you like best about traveling by airplane? What do you like least about airplane travel?

Mr. Kim is traveling from Dallas, Texas to San Francisco, California today. He has a ticket for Flight #30 at 8:00 A.M. This flight will take him to Denver, where he will take another plane to San Francisco. It is now 7:30 A.M. and Mr.

Kim is waiting for his flight. First, you will hear a short airport announcement. Then, you will hear a conversation between Mr. Kim and a ticket agent.

AIRPORT ANNOUNCEMENT

Attention all Sunset Airline passengers. Flight #30 has been cancelled due to bad weather. Repeat. Attention all Sunset Airline passengers. Flight #30 has been cancelled due to bad weather. Please **see a Sunset Airline ticket agent about** making other flight arrangements. Thank you.

TICKET AGENT: Okay everyone, we'll try to find new flights for all of you as soon as possible. Please come up to the counter **one at a time.** Sir, do you have a ticket for Flight #30?

MR. KIM: Yes, I do, and I *must* be in San Francisco this afternoon. I have a very important business meeting to go to.

TICKET AGENT: Let's see what I can do for you. What time do you need to be in San Francisco?

MR. KIM: My meeting starts **at 3:00 P.M. sharp,** so my flight has to arrive by 2:00 P.M. This is terrible! How can you cancel a flight **at the last minute?**

TICKET AGENT: I'm sorry, sir. There's a snowstorm in Denver and the airport is closed there. All flights to that area have been cancelled. We're doing the best we can **under the circumstances.**

MR. KIM: I understand that, but people are **counting on me** to be at this meeting.

TICKET AGENT: I found a seat on our Flight #2, but you'll be stopping in San Diego and Los Angeles. It does arrive in San Francisco at 1:00 P.M. It's all I have right now. Would you like to take that?

MR. KIM: Well, I guess **as a last resort** I'll take it. I have to get there **no matter what.**

TICKET AGENT: Here's your new ticket. That flight leaves in 15 minutes from Gate 3, so go quickly. It's going to be **a close call,** but you can make it. Good luck and have a nice flight.

Getting the Picture...

1. What is the problem with Flight #30?
2. What should the passengers with a ticket for Flight #30 do?

3. Why does Mr. Kim have to be in San Francisco this afternoon? What time does he have to be there?
4. How do you think Mr. Kim feels about this problem?
5. Which new flight will Mr. Kim take?
6. Are there any problems with this new flight?
7. Do you think Mr. Kim was able to get to the plane? Why or why not?

Figuring It Out...

In each sentence below you will find one of the idioms from the conversation. Look at how each idiom is used in the conversation and in the sentence in this exercise. Then try to guess the meaning of each idiom. Write the meaning on the line below each sentence.

1. If you want to change your class, you'll have to **see Mr. Martin about** that because he is the director of this program.

   see (someone) about something _____

2. You may ask your questions **one at a time.** I can't understand you if you all speak at the same time.

   one at a time _____

3. You must be here for the bus **at 6:00 P.M. sharp.** If you are not here then, the bus will leave without you.

   at (time) sharp _____

4. Roland writes all of his reports **at the last minute.** He never does any of his work early.

   at the last minute _____

5. Billy is sick today and must rest in bed. **Under the circumstances,** he cannot go to the birthday party this afternoon.

   under the circumstances _____

6. Pascal comes to every office party. You can **count on him** to be there tonight.

   count on someone _____

7. My car is in the repair shop, and my parents are using their car tonight. **As a last resort,** we can take the bus to the concert tonight.

   as a last resort _____

8. The post office says the mail carrier will deliver the mail **no matter what.** That means the mail will be delivered every day, even in rain or snow.

    no matter what _____

9. Yesterday Peter almost had an accident on the freeway. Another car pulled in front of him just as Peter was exiting, and it was **a** very **close call.**

    a close call _____

Learning the Ins and Outs ....

see about something/see someone about something/see someone about doing something

When you **see about something,** you find out some information or ask about something.

Example: Channel 10 is not working well on my television. Maybe the problem is just with that station. I'll **see about the other stations.**

When you **see someone about something,** you need to name or refer to a specific person. This is the person you are asking the information of.

Example: I'd like to go to the baseball game tomorrow. I'll **see George about the tickets;** I think he has a few extras.

You can also use this idiom with a verb when you want to say you will find out about doing something. In this case, you must add "ing" to the verb.

Example: I'd like to go to the baseball game tomorrow. I'll **see George about getting the tickets.** He always gets them at a discount.

count on someone/something

This idiom means that you can be sure about something or you can rely on something or someone. Be sure to add the person or thing that you can rely on.

Examples: You can always **count on Roger** when you need a ride to school.

You can **count on him** when you need a ride to school.

You can **count on that airline** when you want to have a good flight.

Catching On ....

CHOOSE THE MEANING

Choose the letter of the word or expression that has the same meaning as the italicized idiom in the sentence. In each case you should find two correct answers.

1. Andrea is having trouble reading signs on the road at night. She'll *see the eye doctor about* getting glasses.
   a. check with the eye doctor about
   b. write a letter to the eye doctor about
   c. ask the eye doctor about

2. I'll be happy to answer your questions *one at a time*.
   a. all together
   b. individually
   c. first one and then the next

3. You must arrive for your appointment *at 6:00 P.M. sharp*.
   a. at about 6:00 P.M.
   b. promptly at 6:00 P.M.
   c. exactly at 6:00 P.M.

4. It's too late to change your grade on the paper, because you gave it to me *at the last minute*.
   a. very late
   b. at the last possible time
   c. too early

5. You have reached your limit on your charge card. *Under the circumstances* you cannot charge anything else this month.
   a. because of this
   b. in this situation
   c. before this situation

6. You can always *count on* Jean Paul to score a goal. He's the best player on the soccer team.
   a. forget about
   b. rely on
   c. depend on

7. I can't find a place that delivers some pizza. *As a last resort,* I guess I could run out and get the food.
   a. if all else fails
   b. as a first choice
   c. as a last choice

8. Do you think you'll go home for the holidays? I always see my family then, *no matter what.*
    a. not important
    b. in any situation or case
    c. regardless of everything else

9. My mother came home just after I made an expensive long-distance telephone call. That was *a close call.*
    a. a secret telephone call
    b. almost a problem
    c. a narrow escape

LISTENING

You are going to listen to several short conversations. After each one, you will hear a question. Find the best answer for each question. Circle the letter of your answer.

Part A

1. a. She is not sure about it.
    b. She is sure Mrs. Smith cannot babysit.
    c. She is sure Mrs. Smith will be available.

2. a. He's going to wait another 15 minutes and then ask the hostess.
    b. He's going to wait as long as necessary because he doesn't like to talk to the hostess.
    c. He's going to find the hostess and ask her about their table right away.

3. a. She doesn't want them to answer individually.
    b. She doesn't want them all to speak at the same time.
    c. She doesn't want them to raise their hands.

4. a. The customer broke the bowl with the child.
    b. The manager wasn't watching the child very carefully.
    c. The customer wasn't watching the child very carefully.

5. a. He's been sick for several days.
    b. He just got sick a little while ago.
    c. He's planning on coming later.

6. a. at 6:00 P.M.
    b. at 6:25 P.M.
    c. at 6:30 P.M.

Part B

1. a. He will ask him as a last resort.
    b. He will never ask him, even as a last resort.
    c. As a last resort, he will ask someone else.

2. a. It's no matter to her. She thinks the meeting is not important enough.
    b. She wants to go, but she cannot make it no matter what.
    c. She has many things to do, but she'll be there no matter what.

3. a. She had a close call with the car making the illegal U turn.
    b. She had a close call at the stop sign.
    c. She thought she was getting a ticket. It was a close call.

Holding Your Own ....

Below you will find an advertisement from a travel agency and a conversation with blank spaces. Fill in each of the blanks with one of the idioms below. You will not use all of the idioms, but you will need to use some idioms more than one time. Some spaces may have more than one possible answer. Be sure to make any changes in the idioms to agree with the rest of the sentence.

•see about	•as a last resort	•at the last minute
•count on	•one at a time	•at 10:00 A.M. sharp
•no matter what	•a close call	•under the circumstances

VACATION IN ACAPULCO WITH COLEMAN TOURS

This winter, spend a fabulous week in Acapulco with Coleman Tours. You can

_____ Coleman for the most luxurious vacation packages at the most rea-

sonable prices. Call any of our three locations to _____ making reserva-

tions NOW. It's never too early! All of our offices open _____ seven days a

week.

THE LOST LUGGAGE

Jorge has just arrived at Kennedy Airport in New York City, and he can't find his luggage. He has just gone to the lost baggage office.

JORGE: Excuse me, I'm here to _____ my luggage. I arrived on Flight 52 about 45 minutes ago, but my luggage hasn't come out yet.

CLERK: Could you fill out this paper, please? I'm afraid our computers are down right now. _____ it might take a little time to find your luggage.

JORGE: Oh, great! I have to be at a wedding _____, and all of my clothes are in that luggage.

CLERK: I'm very sorry, sir. We'll do everything we can to find your things. And if we can't find them, we'll give you some money to buy a few new things. _____ you can buy some new clothes for the wedding.

JORGE: What! I can't go out and buy new formal clothes _____ _____. No, I have to get *my* luggage with *my* clothes _____.

CLERK: Oh, here comes someone carrying two pieces of luggage. Could those be yours?

JORGE: Yes, those are my bags. Thank goodness. That was such _____!

WHAT WOULD YOU SAY?

Complete each of the following conversations using the idiom given in parentheses. In some cases you will write a question, and in other cases you will write a response. You should write a question only on the lines with question marks. All of your other answers should be affirmative sentences.

1. A: My car is in the repair shop again. This is the third time in two months.

    B: _____

    (see about)

2. A: Are you definitely coming to the class picnic at the park next weekend?

    _____?

    (count on someone)

    B: Sure, I'll make the salad and a dessert.

3. A: Why are you late? You didn't have an accident with my car, did you?

   B: _____

   (a close call)

4. A: We don't usually like to take checks at this restaurant. _____

   _____

   (under the circumstances)

   B: Thank you so much. Next time I'll remember to bring cash.

5. A: When can we give you the test papers?

   B: _____

   (one at a time)

6. A: My big research report is due tomorrow. I'll never get it done.

   B: _____

   (as a last resort)

7. A: Why are you staying up so late? It's time to go to bed now.

   B: _____

   (no matter what)

8. A: What time does the new math class begin?

   B: _____

   (at time sharp)

9. A: _____?

   (at the last minute)

   B: Yes, we did. Ed had to work last weekend, so we couldn't go to Las Vegas. We'll try to go another time.

Wrapping It Up ....

Your teacher will assign partners. One of you will be PARTNER A and the other will be PARTNER B. If you are PARTNER A, read only the information under PARTNER A and follow the instructions given. If you are PARTNER B, read only the information under PARTNER B and follow the instructions given. Be prepared to share your conversation with the rest of the class at the end of this activity.

Partner A
••••••••••

You work at a very busy travel agency. It's lunchtime, and you and your boss are the only workers in the office right now. There are five customers, and your boss is talking on the telephone right now.

Your partner is one of the customers. Today is Wednesday, and s/he wants to change some travel plans for this Friday. S/he wants to be helped quickly because s/he must get back to work in 15 minutes. Other customers want you to help them also.

Here is the information you will need about your partner's travel arrangements:

Plane Flights: Leave—Friday—Los Angeles to Mexico City
                  Return—Thursday—Mexico City to Los Angeles
                  Cost—$200—special rate for a direct flight—costs another $100 if any stops between Los Angeles and Mexico City
Hotel: Hilton—$85 a night—rate changes to $100 a night if less than five nights

Try to help your customer with his/her problem, using as many of the idioms from this lesson as possible.

Partner B
. . . .

You have planned a trip to Mexico City, to leave this Friday and to return next Thursday. Today is Wednesday, and you have decided you want to change your plans. You are now on your lunch break, and you are at the travel agency. It is very busy; there are several other customers. You only have about 15 minutes and then you must return to work.

Here are the changes you want to make in your travel plans:

- You don't want to stay in Mexico City until next Thursday.
- You want to leave Mexico City on Tuesday and go to San Diego.
- You want to stay in San Diego until Thursday and then return to Los Angeles
- You don't want to spend any more money than you have already planned to spend.

Discuss this situation with your partner (the travel agent), using as many of the idioms from this lesson as possible.

Talking It Over..

1. Have you ever had a close call when you were traveling on a bus, train, or airplane? Tell the class about your experience.
2. In your country, is arriving on time considered important? Do most people usually arrive sharply at the appointed time, late, or early for the following events?
   - a Saturday night party at a friend's house
   - a dinner part at a friend's house
   - a business meeting
   - a wedding
3. Do you ever prepare for things at the last minute? If so, what kinds of things do you prepare for this way?

LESSON 12
Review: Lessons 7-11

I. CROSSWORD PUZZLE #1

All of the idioms in the following crossword puzzle contain two words and are found in lessons 7–11 in this book.

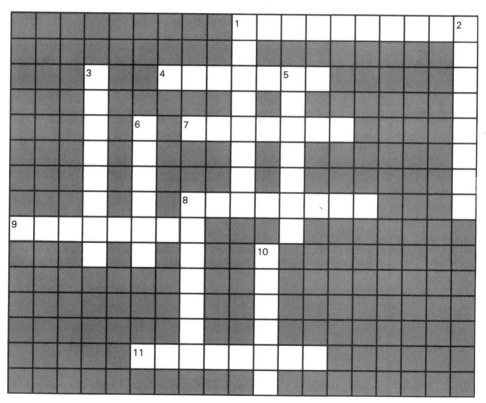

Across
1. reduce spending
4. wealthy
7. in the beginning
8. leave
9. be positive
11. cooperate with

Down
1. nervous
2. begin
3. it's not surprising
5. permanently
6. get something
8. lose one's way
10. continue

II. CROSSWORD PUZZLE #2

All of the idioms in the following crossword puzzle contain three words and are found in lessons 7–11 in this book.

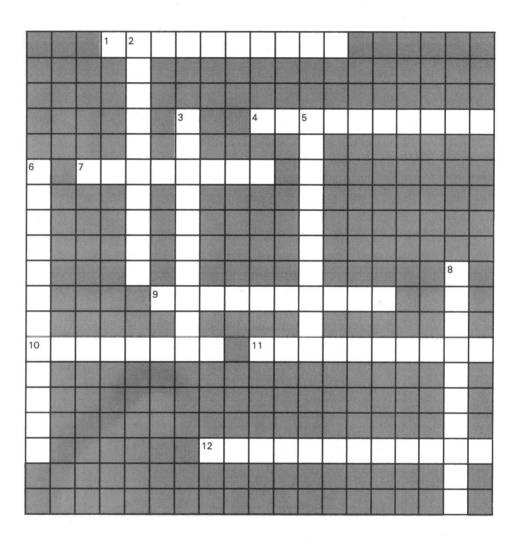

Across
1. turn right
4. narrow escape
7. I have some extra information
9. go at the same speed
10. use it all up
11. far in front
12. first one way, then the other

Down
2. constantly
3. be comfortable with
5. be the leader
6. in any situation
8. have a problem

III. MATCHING

Match the idioms in the column on the left with their meanings in the column on the right. Put the letter of the meaning next to each number on the left. You will not use all of the meanings.

___	1. at the last minute	a.	have a deadline
___	2. can't believe one's eyes	b.	reach many areas
___	3. cover a lot of ground	c.	forget to call
___	4. find one's way around	d.	take first place easily
___	5. give it your best shot	e.	the last possible time
___	6. let someone know	f.	make an effort
___	7. play it by ear	g.	give a tour
___	8. race against time	h.	very surprised at what one sees
___	9. show someone around	i.	move easily through the area
___	10. take the trouble to	j.	do something without a plan
___	11. win by a mile	k.	try your best
		l.	tell someone

IV. MEANINGS

Next to each number below you will find several words or expressions. In each group there is one that has a different meaning from the others. Find the one that has the different meaning and put a circle around it.

Example:

little	(big)	small	tiny

1. a last choice | if everything else fails | a final exam | as a last resort
2. at a later time | promptly at that time | at that exact time | at (time) sharp
3. count on | put a number on it | rely on | depend on
4. pay for | look for | watch for | keep an eye out for
5. keep your eye on | wear glasses | take care of | watch
6. all at one time | individually | one at a time | first one, then the next, etc.

7. ask about   see about   check on   forget about

8. because of this   in this situation   below this   under the circumstances

V. LISTENING PRACTICE

Listen to the questions for this exercise. Then write an answer to each question. You must use one of the idioms given in parentheses in your answer. You may need to write two sentences (to explain the situation) for some answers. If possible, give more than one answer, using a different idiom each time.

1. (keep an eye out for/keep on/make a right)

_____

_____

_____

_____

2. (cut corners/feel free to)

_____

_____

_____

_____

3. (under the circumstances/keep up with/way ahead of)

_____

_____

_____

_____

4. (win by a mile/at first/lead the way)

_____

_____

_____

_____

5.   (as a last resort/see someone about/no matter what)

VI. DICTATION AND ANSWER

For this exercise you will do two things:

A.   First, you will hear some questions. Write these questions in the spaces next to the numbers below.

B.   After all of the questions have been written down, answer each one. Each of your answers must include one of the idioms listed below. Use a different idiom in each answer. (You will not use all of the idioms.)

•play it by ear	•count on someone	•get lost
•in hot water	•a close call	•show someone around
•run out of	•at the last minute	•give it one's best shot
•cold feet	•let someone know	•make sure
•start out	•at (time) sharp	•race against time

1.   --
     ---?

     ----

2.   --
     ---?

     ----

3.   --
     ---?

     ----

4. _____

   _____?

   _____

   _____

5. _____

   _____?

   _____

   _____

VII. PROBLEM SOLVING—THE ENVIRONMENT

PROBLEM
There are many environmental problems in the world today, such as air and water pollution, too much garbage/waste, energy problems, etc. With your classmates, discuss and make a list of as many different types of environmental problems as you can think of. Try to use as many of the following idioms as you can in your sentences.

IDIOMS

- in hot water
- race against time
- can't believe one's eyes

- no wonder
- for good
- run out of

- one at a time
- a close call

SENTENCES ABOUT PROBLEMS

1. _____
2. _____
3. _____
4. _____
5. _____
6. _____
7. _____
8. _____
9. _____
10. _____

SOLUTIONS

What can each person do (as an individual) to try to help solve some of these problems? Your teacher will assign you a partner or put the class into small groups. With your partner or group, discuss some possible solutions to these problems. Write your answers on the lines below, using as many of the idioms given below as possible. Try to think of as many solutions as possible. Be prepared to share your answers with the rest of the class.

IDIOMS

- start out (by)
- make sure
- keep up with
- under the circumstances

- keep one's eye out for
- at all times
- lead the way
- as a last resort

- keep on
- take the trouble to
- cut corners
- no matter what

SENTENCES ABOUT SOLUTIONS

1. _____
2. _____
3. _____
4. _____
5. _____
6. _____
7. _____
8. _____
9. _____
10. _____
11. _____
12. _____

VIII. IDIOM GAME SHOW

Have you ever watched game shows on television? Have you ever wanted to be on one of these shows? Here's your chance to show how much you know about the idioms we have studied in lessons 7 through 11.

This game can be played individually or in groups. Your teacher will decide how your class will play. If you play individually, each student should write the answers in the boxes below. If you play with a partner or in groups or teams, each pair or group should try to find the answers together and write them in the boxes below.

Look at the game board below. You will see numbers on the left. These numbers tell you how many points you will get for the correct answers. At the top of the board, you will see categories. These tell you what kind of idiom you will be asked about. (For example, in the column called "body parts," each question or answer will refer to a part of the body.)

Your teacher will give each person, pair, group, or team a chance to choose the category and number of points he/she/they wish to try. Then your teacher will tell you some information or ask a question about the idiom. You must try to give the correct answer. If you are correct, you will get the points. If you are not correct, you will get no points. You will take turns with the other people in your class to try to answer the questions, and the game will continue until all of the questions have been answered. The questions for 10 points are the easiest, and the questions for 50 points are the most difficult. GOOD LUCK!!

	2 Words	3 Words	Body Parts	Begins with "Get" or "Make"	Words with "Time"
10 points					
20 points					
30 points					
40 points					
50 points					

IX. STORY GO 'ROUND

Look at the picture below. Your class is going to tell a story about what's happening in the picture. The teacher will ask one student to begin the story. This student must use one of the idioms we have reviewed in this lesson. Then the teacher will stop this student and ask another student to continue the story. This student must also use one of the idioms we have reviewed in this lesson. The teacher will continue to ask different students to continue the story. Each student must try to use a different idiom when s/he adds to the story.

Teacher's Script

LESSON 1

Getting Your Feet Wet -Instructions...............

My name is Lisa Cross. That's spelled c as in cat, r as in Robert, o, double s. While I'm in New York, I'll be living with my uncle. The address is 25 Lake Street, New York, New York 11372. I can't remember the phone number. Oh, wait. I think I wrote it down. Here it is. It's 718-335-1799. Do you need any other information? My birthdate? It's March 5, 1970.

Catching On...

LISTENING

Part A

1. MAN: Excuse me, Ms. Winston, are you in charge of Customer Service at this store?

   WOMAN: No I'm not. That would be Mrs. Rubino. Could *I* help you?

   Who is the supervisor of Customer Service at this store?

2. WOMAN: Hi, Andrea. Could you take care of my daughter this afternoon while I go out?

   GIRL: Sure, I'll be glad to. How long will you be gone?

   What does the woman want Andrea to do?

3. CUSTOMER: Could I change my order? I just want the sandwich and not the soup.

   WAITER: I've just handed in your order, sir. I'm not sure if I can change it now. I'll ask the cook.

   Why isn't the waiter sure if he can change the man's order?

4. MAN: Excuse me. Could you tell me a little bit about this new computer you have on sale?

   WOMAN: Certainly, sir. This is our most up-to-date model. Come with me and I'll show you how it works.

   What kind of computer is the man looking at?

5. BOY: Mr. Price, may I leave work early today? My parents are arriving at the airport at 5:00 P.M. and I'd like to meet them.

    MAN: As a rule, I don't like to do this. If you can get all your work done before you leave, you can go.

How does Mr. Price feel about letting workers leave early from work?

Part B

1. WOMAN: I'm calling about my subscription to your magazine. I cancelled it last month, but I received a new bill from you yesterday.

    MAN: You need to speak to our service representative. I'll connect you.

    Why is this woman calling the magazine office?

2. GIRL: I'm here to take the English language test. Can I have the papers to register now?

    WOMAN: I'm sorry. You're too late. You had to register for the test last week.

    When did the girl have to register for the English test?

3. WOMAN: How can I order this clock from your catalogue?

    MAN: First, you need to complete this paper. Then you need to give it to me, and I'll help you with the order.

    What must the woman do first?

4. WOMAN: Hey, Greg. Where were you last night? You didn't come to the party.

    MAN: I know. I didn't write it down in my appointment book and I forgot all about it.

    Why did the man forget about the party?

More Listening / Pronunciation Practice........

I. LISTEN AND REPEAT

Listen to the pronunciation of each of the idioms from this lesson. Then say the idiom out loud after each one is said on the tape.

(be) in charge of
clear up
hand in
fill out
take care of

in advance
up-to-date
as a rule
make a note of

II. LISTENING—CONTRACTIONS

Contractions are short forms. Often when native speakers talk, they combine two words together into one word. This word is called a contraction. This often happens with the subject of a sentence and an auxiliary that follows the subject (such as am/is/are/have/will).

For example: **I am** becomes **I'm.**
I'm registering for that class today.

I have becomes **I've.**
I've already registered for that class.

I will becomes **I'll.**
I'll register for that class next week.

When **have** is used as a main verb, we do *not* make the contraction.

For example: **I have** some questions about this class.

In this exercise, you will practice listening to contractions with the auxiliaries **be** (am/is/are), **have**, and **will**. As you listen, write down all the contractions you hear. You will hear only one sentence after each number. Then you will have some time to write your answers. In some cases, you may not hear any contractions. Just write NONE if this is the case.

After each number, you will hear the sentence repeated two times.

Example: You're going to take a two-week class for managers.

1. You've just arrived at the school to begin the course.
2. My name is Edna Monroe and I'm in charge of registration.
3. I'll try to clear up any questions you may have.
4. To complete this registration, you'll need to do two things.
5. You'll see Mrs. Wong at the computer so that you can take care of payment.
6. Some of you've paid in advance.
7. Mrs. Wong needs to make sure your account's completely up-to-date.
8. Please speak to Mrs. Wong if you have any questions about this.

9. There's one change in the schedule for this afternoon.
10. The 2:00 P.M. class will meet in Room 16, not in Room 10.
11. I've written this information on the blackboard behind me.
12. Now, if you've completed all of your papers, please see Mr. Bils.

III. PRONUNCIATION—CONTRACTIONS

Now, repeat each contraction after you hear it.

you're
you've
I'm
I'll
you'll
account's
there's
I've

LESSON 2

Catching On...

LISTENING

Part A

1. Isabella asked her brother for some money. He said, "To tell you the truth, I don't have any right now."
2. Bettina's going to order that new magazine because they have an early bird special for new orders this month.
3. Bill has cancelled his trip to Miami this weekend; the trip is out of the question.
4. Bob says he can't go to the movies with us tonight because he's broke.
5. When Oliver told his wife he was unhappy with their new car, she said, "That makes two of us."

Part B

1. Janet is sick in bed with a fever today.
2. The waiter is taking everyone's dinner order at Sandy's table.
3. George needs to buy a car, but he doesn't have much money.
4. Steve worked very late last night, and then he went out to dinner.
5. Minoru wants to take the subway home, but the subway is closed.

More Listening / Pronunciation Practice........

I. LISTEN AND REPEAT

Listen to the pronunciation of each of the idioms from this lesson. Then say the idiom out loud after each one is said on the tape.

> make up one's mind
>
> feel like
>
> to tell you the truth
>
> be broke
>
> that makes two of us
>
> out of the question
>
> early bird special
>
> find out

II. LISTENING—REDUCED FORMS

In Lesson 1, you learned about short forms called contractions. Sometimes in conversation, you will hear native speakers say their words quickly in another way. In this case, they put words together to make another kind of shortened form, called reduced forms. These forms are not real words. You will never find them in writing. They are used only in conversation.

Here are some examples of reduced forms found in the conversation at the restaurant in Lesson 2:

Form	Comes From	Example
ya	you	How are **ya?**
whaddya	what do you	**Whaddya** think about this?
dya	do you	**Dya** think this is easy?
hadda	had to	She **hadda** go to the doctor this morning.
hafta	have to	I **hafta** finish my homework soon.
outta	out of	I got 5 **outta** 6 correct on the test.
dunno	don't know	I **dunno** the answer.

Listen again to parts of the conversation in the restaurant from this lesson. As you listen, try to find the reduced forms given above. Write down each of the forms above each time you hear one. After each number you will hear a few sentences from the conversation. These sentences will be repeated two times.

1. Well, whaddya feel like eating? Dya want some steak or roast beef?
2. To tell ya the truth, those dinners are too expensive. I hadda fix my car last week, and now I'm almost broke.

3. That makes two of us. I hafta buy a new refrigerator. A steak dinner is outta the question for me.
4. What time is it? There's an early bird special until 6 o'clock. Ya get chicken, rice, a vegetable, and coffee for only $6.99.
5. It's 6 o'clock right now. Dya think we can still get it?
6. I dunno. We can find out from the waitress. Here she comes now.

III. PRONUNCIATION—REDUCED FORMS

Now, repeat each reduced form after you hear it.

ya

whaddya

dya

hadda

hafta

outta

dunno

LESSON 3

Getting Your Feet Wet -Questions ....

1. How many people did you see standing in this picture?
2. What is the police officer doing?
3. How many stop lights did you see?
4. What kind of business is in the background?
5. What emergency vehicle did you see in this picture?

Catching On ....

LISTENING

Example:

A. John is not very happy today.
B. John is sad today.

1. A. Susan's boss will be arriving soon, and he wants to see her right away.
    B. Susan's boss is coming to work soon, but she probably won't have time to see him today.

2. A. One of the runners began the race too early.
    B. Runner #12 jumped the gun at the start of the race.

3. A. Sylvie and I both think her teacher will believe her story about her homework.
    B. I just heard Sylvie's excuse about her homework, and I don't think she has a leg to stand on.

4. A. That's an advanced ski slope, so take it easy when you go down that hill.
    B. Since you're an advanced skier, you can go down that ski slope as fast as you like.

5. A. You need to pay attention to my instructions so you'll be able to find my house.
    B. You should listen carefully to me if you want to find my house easily.

6. A. Carlos brought the cat to his house because he pitied the animal.
    B. Carlos felt sorry for the poor lost cat, so he took the cat home with him.

7. A. It was a beautiful morning at the beach and then, all of a sudden, dark clouds came in and it began to rain.
    B. It was a beautiful day all day yesterday until late at night when it rained.

8. A. I know Ann too. Actually, she was a classmate of mine.
    B. Yes, I know Ann. In fact, she was in my history class last year.

More Listening/Pronunciation Practice.......

I. LISTEN AND REPEAT

Listen to the pronunciation of each of the idioms from this lesson. Then say the idiom out loud after each one is said on the tape.

right away
in fact
all of a sudden
have a leg to stand on
jump the gun
feel sorry for
take it easy
pay attention to

II. LISTENING—MORE REDUCED FORMS AND *S* AND *Z* SOUNDS

A. More Reduced Forms

Here are two other examples of reduced forms:

1. At the end of the **ing** form of a verb, native speakers often drop the **g.**
   Example: I'm **takin'** the 5 o'clock train.
2. The word **to** often becomes **ta.**
   Example: I like **ta** read mystery books.

Listen to Witness #1's story from this lesson again. Write down the words you hear that are **ing** words but are pronounced without the end g sound. Listen for the **ta** sounds as well. How many times did you hear the **ta** after each number? The sentences will be repeated two times after each number.

1. I saw the truck comin' down College Avenue.
2. Right away I noticed it was travelin' too fast.
3. In fact, I heard someone yell ta the driver ta slow down.
4. Then, just as the yellow light was turnin' red, he started ta go faster.
5. I guess the driver of the blue car didn't see the truck speedin' up at the intersection.
6. When the car started ta make a left turn, it went right inta the truck.

B. Practice with Sounds—S/Z

Sometimes in English the letter s is pronounced like an s as in **see.** Other times the letter s is pronounced like a z as in **times.** The z pronunciation is often found at the end of a word.

Turn back to Witness #3's story at the beginning of this lesson. You are going to hear this story again. Look for words with the letter s and listen for the s and z sounds. If you hear the s sound, circle the word with the s that makes this sound. If you hear the z sound, put a line under the word with the s that makes this sound.

I feel sorry for the driver of the car. He waited for the green light to make his left turn. He was taking it easy going through the intersection and BANG! Just then the truck came flying across the road. The driver of the truck wasn't paying attention to the changing light. I sure hope he has good insurance.

III. Pronunciation—Reduced Forms / *S* and *Z* Sounds

Now, repeat each reduced form after you hear it.

> comin'
> travelin'
> turnin'
> speedin'
> ta
> inta

Now, repeat each word after you hear it.

> sorry
> his
> was
> easy
> intersection
> just
> across
> wasn't
> has

LESSON 4

Catching On..

LISTENING

Part A

1. Sally invited me to drop by her new house any time this week.
2. Raul is very disappointed. He wanted to go to Harvard next year, but the school turned him down.
3. Carl is going to Los Angeles for the weekend. He'll get in touch with Liz after he returns.
4. Mark didn't know if he should lend Gary his car last night. Gary said, "C'mon, Mark I'll be back before 11 PM and I'll return the car to you then."
5. Do you think I can get more time to finish my paper for this class?

It's up to Dr. Johns. He's the only one who can change the date for an assignment.

Part B

1. Jim is very stubborn and always thinks his opinion is the correct one.
2. It rained last night, so the baseball game was cancelled and everyone had to go home.
3. Charles didn't want to go out last night. Then he talked to Alice and he decided to see a movie with her.
4. Ilaria said, "I don't want to cook dinner tonight. I feel like eating pizza, so let's eat at that new Italian restaurant."

More Listening / Pronunciation Practice........

I. LISTEN AND REPEAT

Listen to the pronunciation of each of the idioms from this lesson. Then say the idiom out loud after each one is said on the tape.

drop by

take a rain check

talk someone into something

in the mood for

come on

turn someone down

up to someone

change one's mind

get in touch with

II. LISTENING—INTONATION—QUESTIONS

When asking a question in English, native speakers change the tone of their voice. The tone (or pitch) of a sentence goes up at the end.

Examples: Can I see you tonight?

Are you busy tomorrow?

After each number you will hear two sentences, **A** and **B**. One will be a question and the other will not. Write the letter of the sentence (**A** or **B**) that you think is a question. Listen carefully to the intonation.

1. A. Betty would like to join me.
   B. Betty, would you like to join me?

2. A. Can I take a rain check?
   B. I can take a rain check.

3. A. Carmen, do you have any plans for tonight?
   B. Carmen has no plans for tonight.

4. A. Why don't you come with me?
   B. I don't know why you came with me.

5. A. I don't like science fiction.
   B. Do you like science fiction?

6. A. I'm sure you can't talk me into coming with you.
   B. Are you sure I can't talk you into coming with me?

7. A. What about you, Rudy?
   B. I forgot all about Rudy.

III. PRONUNCIATION—QUESTIONS

Now, repeat each question after you hear it.

1. Betty, would you like to join me?
2. Can I take a rain check?
3. Carmen, do you have any plans for tonight?
4. Why don't you come with me?
5. Do you like science fiction?
6. Are you sure I can't talk you into coming with me?
7. What about you, Rudy?

LESSON 5

Catching On..

LISTENING

Department Store Announcement

Attention shoppers! Be sure to take advantage of our one-hour special sale today. At 2:00 P.M. we will be selling our gold jewelry at 10 percent off. That's right. Believe it nor not, in 15 minutes ALL of our gold earrings, bracelets, necklaces, and more will be on sale for one hour only. So don't put off coming to our jewelry department between 2:00 and 3:00 P.M. today.

Jenny's New Car: Part One

I must tell you the story about my sister Jenny's new car. Two weeks ago, she decided her old car was on its last legs and she needed a new one. She didn't want to pay an arm and a leg, so she decided to buy a used car. She found a small car that looked almost new, and it only had 20,000 miles on it. The best part was, believe it or not, it only cost $2,000! She thought the salesman was pulling her leg when he told her the price. He told her he was calling it quits and moving his business to Los Angeles. That's why it was so cheap. So, Jenny bought the car.

Jenny's New Car: Part Two

Did I tell you what happened to Jenny's new car? I think she bought a lemon. Last week she had to fix her headlights because they weren't working right. Then, yesterday, the car started making a funny noise. She tried to take it back to the car dealer, but the business was gone! So she took it to a mechanic and he said it was a problem with the engine. Now she has to spend $300 on repairs. In other words, she saved some money when she bought a cheap car, but now she's paying an arm and a leg on repairs! That salesman really took advantage of her.

More Listening / Pronunciation Practice.......

I. LISTEN AND REPEAT

Listen to the pronunciation of each of the idioms from this lesson. Then say the idiom out loud after each one is said on the tape.

on one's last legs

pay an arm and a leg

a lemon

call it quits

take advantage of

believe it or not

in other words

pull someone's leg

put off

II. LISTENING—*TH/CH/SH* SOUNDS

A. *TH* Sounds

There are many words in English with the **th** spelling. The **th** can make more than one sound. Listen to the following examples:

This is the most interesting story.

Nothing can stop us.

You are going to hear some sentences from the advertisement at the beginning of this lesson again. You will find these sentences below. Put a line under any word with the **th** sound as in nothing. Put a circle around any word with the **th** sound as in the. You will hear each sentence two times.

1. This is Mark Shark from the Shark Discount Appliance Center.
2. That's right, folks.
3. Starting November 5th I'll have the lowest prices in town.
4. Take advantage of this exciting sale.
5. Everything in the store will be half price!
6. If you come with cash, we'll give you another 10 percent.
7. In other words, you'll get 60 percent savings.

B. *CH/SH* Sounds

Listen to the **ch** and **sh** sounds in the following examples:

We should be home at about 6:00 P.M.

Do you have change for a dollar?

Now listen to some of the sentences from the advertisement from this lesson one more time. This time put an X on any word with the **ch** sound. Put a check on any word with the **sh** sound. You will hear each sentence two times.

1. Is your dishwasher a lemon?
2. This is Mark Shark from the Shark Discount Appliance Center.
3. If you come with cash, we'll give you another 10 percent.
4. You'll get 50 percent when you pay with a check or charge card.

III. PRONUNCIATION—*TH/CH/SH*

Now, repeat each word after you hear it.

this
the
that
5th
everything
with
another
other
dishwasher
shark
cash
check
charge

LESSON 6

V. Listening Practice ....

1. What did she tell her husband while he was driving?
2. Why does Joe look so unhappy today?
3. How did you break your arm?
4. Why is John nervous about telling his mother about the lost diamond ring?
5. I'm confused. Do you know how to register for this course?

VI. Dictation and Answer ....

Following are the dictation questions for this exercise.

1. Has she made up her mind about buying a new car?
2. Is your boss going to drop by the office with the report this afternoon?
3. Should we go for the early bird special at the restaurant on the corner?
4. Can I talk you into going to see a movie with me tonight?
5. Why did Sue get in touch with her mother yesterday?

VII. Idiom Game Show ....

QUESTIONS (ANSWERS ARE GIVEN IN PARENTHESES AFTER EACH QUESTION)

2-Words

10 points: I bought a bad product. What did I buy? (a lemon)

20 points: What is the meaning of "find out?" (get information)

30 points: If I say please visit me anytime, what should you do? (drop by)

40 points: You are lazy and you never like to do your work. Probably you often _____ your work. (put off)

50 points: We have a big problem. If we must fix the problem, what must we do? (clear it/the problem up **or** clear up the problem)

3-Words

10 points: What does the idiom "call it quits" mean? (stop/give up)

20 points: What is an early bird special? (discount price at a certain time—especially for meals at a restaurant)

30 points: The baseball game is cancelled because of rain. We can _____. (take a raincheck)

40 points: In general, the teacher doesn't like to accept late homework. What's another way of saying "in general?" (as a rule)

50 points: If I am fooling you or tricking you, I am _____. (pulling your leg)

Body Parts

10 points: What is the meaning of "pay an arm and a leg?" (spend a lot of money)

20 points: If I hand in my paper to the teacher, what do I do? (give it to the teacher)

30 points: I have an old refrigerator in very bad condition. I can say my refrigerator is _____. (on its last legs)

40 points: I was playing with my mother's expensive watch, and I lost it. I'm nervous about telling her what happened. Why? (You don't have a leg to stand on.)

50 points: This morning I wanted to go bowling, but now I've decided to stay home. What did I do when I made this new decision? (You changed your mind.)

Begins with "In"

10 points: What's the meaning of "in fact?" (really/actually)

20 points: What is the meaning of "in other words?" (that is to say/to say it in another way/to explain it in another way)

30 points: Yesterday you did something early. You did it _____. (in advance)

40 points: Jill's boss gave her a new job. She is now a supervisor, so she is _____ her department. (in charge of)

50 points: If you don't feel like doing something, you are probably not _____ to do it. (in the mood)

Begins with "T"

10 points: What is the meaning of "take it easy?" (go slowly/relax)

20 points: This idiom means to use something to your own benefit. (take advantage of)

30 points: Gabriela said no to Jose's invitation. Gabriela _____. (turned him down/turned Jose down)

40 points: When I try to convince you to do something, I try to _____. (talk you into something or into doing something)

50 points: I agree with you, so I might say _____. (that makes two of us)

LESSON 7

Catching On...

LISTENING

1. A. Jose got lost on the subway yesterday morning, so he took a taxi home in the afternoon.

B. Jose took a taxi two times yesterday because he didn't want to get lost on the subway.

2. A. Jack started out on his trip alone, but then his friends joined him in Los Angeles.
B. Jack began traveling without his friends and then they met him later.

3. A. Did you check your wallet to see that you have enough money with you?
B. Make sure you have enough checks in your wallet when you go shopping.

4. A. Sherry didn't know how to fix the copy machine at the office.
B. Sherry took the trouble to fix the copy machine at the office.

5. A. Vu asked a police officer for directions because he couldn't find his way around the city.
B. Vu had trouble getting around the city, and then he asked for help.

6. A. In many places you can make a right at a red light when it is safe.
B. You should not turn right at a red light because it is usually not safe.

7. A. Some of the students continued to talk after the teacher asked for quiet.
B. The teacher asked everyone to be quiet, but a few students kept on talking.

8. A. Janet's plane has just arrived, so keep your eye out for her at the gate.
B. Watch for Janet because she should be getting off the airplane soon.

More Listening / Pronunciation Practice ....

I. LISTEN AND REPEAT

Listen to the pronunciation of each of the idioms from this lesson. Then say the idiom out loud after each one is said on the tape.

find one's way around

start out

keep one's eye out for

keep on

make sure

make a right

take the trouble to

get lost

II. LISTENING—MORE CONTRACTIONS

We have already talked about contractions with the auxiliaries **be, have,** and **will** in Lesson 1. In this lesson, we will review listening to contractions with **be** and **will.** We will also listen to contractions with two other auxiliaries: **can** and **do** in negative situations.

> Examples: I **can't** help you right now.
>
> I **don't** want to help you right now.

Listen to some of the sentences in the conversation about directions from the beginning of this lesson. As you listen, write down all the contractions you hear. You will hear only one or two sentences at a time, and then you will have some time to write your answers. In some cases, you may not hear any contractions. Just write NONE if this is the case. You will hear each sentence repeated two times.

1. I'm trying to find the bookstore, but I can't find my way around this campus.
2. I have a map but I'm still confused.
3. You're looking for the bookstore?
4. That's pretty far away from here. In fact, it's on the other side of campus.
5. We're here, next to the Student Center. You'll start out at these steps.
6. Keep your eye out for the library. It'll be on the left.
7. Just a minute; let me make sure I see that on the map.
8. Just before the cafeteria, you'll make a right.
9. You'll see it right away.
10. I hope I don't get lost again.

III. PRONUNCIATION—CONTRACTIONS

Now, repeat each contraction after you hear it.

I'm
can't
you're
that's
it's
we're
you'll
it'll
don't

LESSON 8

Catching On ....

LISTENING

Postal Worker's Announcement

Attention, please. Be sure to wait in only one line at all times. A clerk will call you as you reach the front of the line. If you are sending an insured package, you must complete an insurance form. Feel free to take a form from the table and complete it while you are waiting to be helped. If you are here to pick up a package, go to the end of the counter with your yellow slip. Thank you.

At the Museum

Please listen carefully, everyone. We're going to cover a lot of ground today because we have three areas to visit. First, we'll see the ancient Greek art on the third floor, then the Roman art on the second floor, and finally, the ancient Egyptian section on the first floor. Please be sure to keep up with the group at all times! We'll be meeting a museum guide on the third floor in a few minutes. I'll lead the way for now. Is everyone ready? Okay, let's get going.

At the Business Meeting

Good morning, everyone. I'm Kathy Mendoza, project manager for the new North City business park. I've prepared a detailed report for you about how we plan to build this park. I'll be covering a lot of ground, so please feel free to stop me to ask questions at any time. You each should have a written report in front of you to help you keep up with me as I talk. Oh, and by the way, this is my assistant, Frank Sforza. He's been helping me prepare this report, so he can answer some questions as well. After this meeting, we'll be happy to show you around the office, so you can see some of the other projects we're working on. Now, if everyone is ready, I think we should begin.

More Listening / Pronunciation Practice ....

I. LISTEN AND REPEAT

Listen to the pronunciation of each of the idioms from this lesson. Then say the idiom out loud after each one is said on the tape.

at all times

by the way

show someone around

feel free to

cover a lot of ground

pick up

keep up with

get going

lead the way

II. LISTENING—SOUNDS OF THE LETTER I

A.   The letter **i** can be pronounced in several ways in English. Listen to the following examples:

This **i**s a b**i**g sh**i**p.

B.   There are other words with this letter that have a different sound. Listen to these examples:

I saw that movie for the second t**i**me last n**i**ght.

Now listen to some of the sentences from the tour guide in this lesson again. (Some parts of it have been changed a little for this exercise.) You will find the sentences below. Listen for the two different sounds of i discussed above. If a word has the first i sound (as in ship), put an X on the letter i. If a word has the second i sound (as in time), put a check on the letter i. (Note: In some cases, a word might have both i sounds.) Each sentence will be said separately and will be repeated two times.

1.   Welcome to the Clover Line afternoon tour.
2.   My name is Robin.
3.   In a few minutes, we'll begin.
4.   I'd like to remind you to stay seated.
5.   Keep your hands inside the bus at all times.
6.   This is our bus driver, Phil.
7.   If you have any questions, please ask me or Phil.
8.   Our tour this afternoon will take three hours.
9.   We will be making a short stop in Chinatown.
10.   You can take pictures and pick up some postcards.

III. PRONUNCIATION—THE LETTER I

Now, repeat each word after you hear it.

I as in **time**	I as in **ship**
line	is
I	Robin
I'd	inside
like	in
remind	minutes
times	this
driver	Phil
Chinatown	begin
inside	if
	will
	making
	pictures
	pick

LESSON 9

Catching On ....

LISTENING

Part A

1. Bill finished way ahead of everyone else on the test.
2. I'll race you to the car; I'm sure I'll win by a mile.
3. You need to keep your eye on the soup to make sure it doesn't boil over.
4. I can't believe my eyes. Is that really the world famous opera singer from Italy?
5. Jorge had to race against time to get to the store before it closed at 6 o'clock.

Part B

1. At 1 o'clock I'll go to the eye doctor. Then I'll order new glasses, and at 6:00 P.M. I have a date with Roger.
2. "Gina, did you break my new expensive glasses?"
   "No, mom, Gregory dropped them this morning."
3. Jack likes his new job, but he thinks he does too much driving from Los Angeles to Riverside every day.
4. This math problem is really hard, but I'll try to do it as best I can.

More Listening / Pronunciation Practice ....

I. LISTEN AND REPEAT

Listen to the pronunciation of each of the idioms from this lesson. Then say the idiom out loud after each one is said on the tape.

> way ahead of
> win by a mile
> keep one's eye on
> at first
> in hot water
> back and forth
> race against time
> can't believe one's eyes
> give it one's best shot

II. LISTENING—INTONATION—EMPHASIS/SURPRISE

Native speakers change the tone of their voice when they want to show surprise or emphasis (making something strong). The tone of the voice will become stronger in these cases. Listen to the following examples:

> She is such a fast runner!
> Lisa has just won the race!

After each number you will hear two sentences, **A** and **B**. In one sentence the speaker will show emphasis or surprise by the tone of voice. In the other sentence, the speaker will not show any emphasis or surprise. Write the letter of the sentence (**A** or **B**) that you think shows emphasis or surprise. Listen carefully to the intonation.

1. **A.** It's Susan Smith in first place!
    B. Susan Smith is in first place.

2. **A.** Here she comes.
    B. Here she comes now!

3. **A.** Paula McCoy has just finished second!
    B. Paula McCoy finished second in the race

4. **A.** What an exciting race!
    B. The race was short but exciting.

5. **A.** Wait a minute for me, please.
    B. Wait a minute!

6.   A.   It's a touchdown for the home team.
     B.   Ladies and gentlemen, it's a touchdown!

III. PRONUNCIATION—EMPHASIS/SURPRISE

Now, repeat each sentence after you hear it. Try to show emphasis or surprise with your intonation.

1.   It's Susan Smith in first place!
2.   Here she comes now!
3.   Paula McCoy has just finished second!
4.   What an exciting race!
5.   Wait a minute!
6.   Ladies and gentlemen, it's a touchdown!

LESSON 10

Catching On...

LISTENING

Part A

1.   Hello, Amy. It's Mom. I still don't know what time the movie starts to-night. I'll call the theater and then I'll call you back.
2.   Amy, this is Marcia. Bret and I had another big fight. He was very angry when he left my apartment and he said he's never going to speak to me again. Please call me.
3.   Hi Amy, it's George. Saturday night's concert has been cancelled. Maybe we could do something else, like listen to music at the Backstreet Cafe. Anyway, I'll pick you up at 6 and we can decide then.
4.   This is Mr. Bixby from Party Time. It's about the big party you're planning for your parents. I'm afraid we won't be able to give you the steak dinner *and* the special flowers *and* the music for $500. For that price, you'll have to leave out something. Let me know what you want to do.
5.   Uh, Amy. It's Bret. Marcia and I had a big fight again. We've been having a lot of problems lately and I thought maybe you could help. Could you call me as soon as you get home? Thanks.

Part B

1.   This is Mindy. It's about those scuba diving lessons we were planning to take together. I'm getting cold feet. Give me a call later and we'll talk about it.

2. Cheryl, this is Peter. I'm sorry I didn't bring the computer paper to your house this morning. I ran out of it yesterday. I'll get a new box tomorrow, so I'll bring you the paper then.

3. Hi, Cheryl. This is Barbara. I can't go with you to the hotel in Palm Springs next weekend. I'm really broke, so I have to work some overtime. Heh heh .. I guess I'm not as well-off as you are. But thanks for the invitation anyway.

4. Hello, Cheryl, this is Eugene from the main office. I just found out you were sick last week. No wonder you didn't come to the party last Friday. I hope you're better now. I'll try to call again later.

More Listening / Pronunciation Practice ....

LISTEN AND REPEAT

Listen to the pronunciation of each of the idioms from this lesson. Then say the idiom out loud after each one is said on the tape.

no wonder

cold feet

get along

for good

cut corners

run out of

well-off

play it by ear

let someone know

II. LISTENING—*E/I* SOUNDS

You have already learned about words with the i sound as in ship. The e sound as in set is sometimes confused with this i sound. Listen to the following examples of the e sound:

Please help me. I don't want to get wet.

Here is a sentence with words that have both the i and the e sounds.

Please put this pin next to my pen.

Now listen to parts of the conversation about the wedding from the beginning of this lesson again. Some of the sentences have been changed a little, so listen carefully. You will see the sentences below. Listen for the **e** and **i** sounds discussed above.

If a word has the **e** sound as in set, put an X on the letter **e**. If a word has the **i** sound as in ship, put a check on the letter **i**. (Some words may have both the **e** and the **i** sounds.) Each sentence will be repeated two times.

1. How was the wedding?
2. It was just beautiful.
3. I don't think so.
4. Those two get along so well.
5. This marriage will be for good.
6. You had dinner at the Grand Hotel, didn't you?
7. It was fantastic!
8. Every time I looked, they brought out another dish.
9. They must be well-off to make such a big affair.
10. Will you need me to babysit?
11. Maybe we'll see you next weekend.
12. I'll let you know.

III. PRONUNCIATION—SHORT E AND SHORT I

Now, repeat each word after you hear it.

E	*I*
wedding	it
get	beautiful
well	think
hotel	this
every	will
next	dinner
weekend	didn't
let	fantastic
	big
	dish
	babysit
	if
	wedding

LESSON 11

Catching On ....

LISTENING

Part A

1. MAN: Do you think Mrs. Smith will be able to babysit for us on Friday night?

    WOMAN: I spoke to her the other day, and she said we could count on her for any weekend.

    Does the woman think Mrs. Smith will be able to babysit?

2. WOMAN: We had reservations for dinner at 7:00 P.M. Haven't we been waiting for a table for a long time?

    MAN: Yes, it's been 15 minutes already. I think I'll see the hostess about it.

    What will the man do?

3. TEACHER: Children, please raise your hand if you think you know the answer. I can only understand you when you speak one at a time. Yes, Barbara?

    BARBARA: Is the answer 53?

    What *doesn't* the teacher want the children to do?

4. CUSTOMER: I'm sorry my little boy broke this glass bowl. He's always touching things in stores.

    MANAGER: We asked you to watch him more carefully. I'm afraid under the circumstances you'll have to pay for the bowl now.

    Why does the manager want the customer to pay for the bowl?

5. WOMAN: Jimmy told me he was coming to the party. Why isn't he here?

    WOMAN: He was planning on being here, but at the last minute he called and said he was sick.

    Why isn't Jimmy at the party?

6. MAN: Where is Ruth? She said she would be here at 6:00 P.M. sharp and it's 6:25 now. The show starts at 6:30.

    WOMAN: You know Ruth. She's always late. Oh, here she comes now.

    What time was Ruth supposed to arrive for the show?

Part B

1. WOMAN: Do you think Bob will be able to work with us on the project?

   MAN: I guess we could ask him, but I know he's very busy. First, can we try to find someone else to help us?

   Does the man want to ask Bob for help?

2. MAN: Will you be able to come to the meeting this afternoon at 3 o'clock?

   WOMAN: Well, I really have a lot of work to do, and I have another meeting at noon. But I'll definitely come to your meeting too.

   What does the woman say about the meeting at 3 o'clock?

3. WOMAN: Uh oh. There's a police car behind me, and he's turning his light on. Didn't I make a complete stop at that stop sign?

   MAN: Sure you did. Look, there's a car making an illegal U turn over there. He's going to stop that driver.

   Why was the woman nervous?

More Listening / Pronunciation Practice........

I. LISTEN AND REPEAT

Listen to the pronunciation of each of the idioms from this lesson. Then say the idiom out loud after each one is said on the tape.

   see someone about
   one at a time
   at 3:00 P.M. sharp
   at the last minute
   under the circumstances
   count on someone
   as a last resort
   no matter what
   a close call

II. LISTENING—NUMBERS

Sometimes listening to numbers in English can be confusing, especially numbers that end in **teen** or **y,** such as **fifteen** and **fifty.**

Listen to the story, airport announcement, and conversation from the beginning of this lesson. Some of the numbers have been changed, so listen carefully. Write down all the numbers you hear.

Mr. Kim is traveling from Dallas, Texas to San Francisco, California today. He has a ticket for Flight #20 at 8:00 A.M. This flight will take him to Denver, where he will take another plane to San Francisco. It is now 7:30 A.M. and Mr. Kim is waiting for his flight. First, you will hear a short airport announcement. Then, you will hear a conversation between Mr. Kim and a ticket agent.

Airport Announcement

Attention all Sunset Airline passengers. Flight #20 has been cancelled due to bad weather. Repeat. Attention all Sunset Airline passengers. Flight #20 has been cancelled due to bad weather. Please see a Sunset Airline ticket agent about making other flight arrangements. Thank you.

TICKET AGENT:	Okay everyone, we'll try to find new flights for all of you as soon as possible. Please come up to the counter one at a time. Sir, do you have a ticket for Flight #20?
MR. KIM:	Yes, I do, and I *must* be in San Francisco this afternoon. I have a very important business meeting to go to.
TICKET AGENT:	Let's see what I can do for you. What time do you need to be in San Francisco?
MR. KIM:	My meeting starts at 3:00 P.M. sharp, so my flight has to arrive by 2:00 P.M. This is terrible! How can you cancel a flight at the last minute?
TICKET AGENT:	I'm sorry, sir. There's a snowstorm in Denver and the airport is closed there. All flights to that area have been cancelled. We're doing the best we can under the circumstances.
MR. KIM:	I understand that, but people are counting on me to be at this meeting.
TICKET AGENT:	I found a seat on our Flight #118, but you'll be stopping in San Diego and Los Angeles. It does arrive in San Francisco at 1:00 P.M. It's all I have right now. Would you like to take that?
MR. KIM:	Well, I guess as a last resort I'll take it. I have to get there no matter what.

TICKET AGENT: Here's your new ticket. That flight leaves in 15 minutes from Gate 23, so go quickly. It's going to be a close call, but you can make it. Good luck and have a nice flight.

III. PRONUNCIATION—NUMBERS

Now, repeat each number after you hear it.

20
8
7:30
3 P.M.
2 P.M.
118
1 P.M.
15
23

LESSON 12

V. Listening Practice ·······························

1. How can I find the new mathematics building?
2. Do you have any chocolate desserts in the kitchen?
3. Why are you walking so fast?
4. What happened at the marathon race yesterday?
5. What will you do about finding a new job?

VI. Dictation and Answer ·······························

Following are the dictation questions for this exercise.

1. Do you know how to find your way around this school?
2. Why were Bob and Sally calling each other back and forth on the telephone yesterday?
3. When will your brother move to Paris for good?
4. Could you take the trouble to show me how to use this machine?
5. What time should we get going for the party?

VII. Idiom Game Show ....

QUESTIONS (ANSWERS ARE GIVEN IN PARENTHESES AFTER EACH QUESTION)

2-Words

10 points: What is the meaning of "keep on?" (continue)

20 points: A wealthy person is _____. (well-off)

30 points: When you begin to do something, you _____. (start out)

40 points: Make a sentence with the idiom "for good."

50 points: If you want to say you are not surprised about something, you might begin your sentence with this idiom. (no wonder)

3-Words

10 points: I ran out of sugar yesterday. What happened? (I used all the sugar or I had no sugar left)

20 points: When you are in trouble, you are _____. (in hot water)

30 points: John almost had an accident with his car. He had _____. (a close call)

40 points: I have some extra information for you. I might start my sentence with this idiom. (by the way)

50 points: Make a sentence with the idiom "feel free to."

Body Parts

10 points: How do I feel when I have cold feet? (nervous)

20 points: What do I do when I keep my eye on something? (I watch it.)

30 points: I am very surprised at what I see. I might say _____. (I can't believe my eyes.)

40 points: I don't want to make any decisions about next weekend. I want to _____. (play it by ear)

50 points: I don't want to get lost. I should _____ the right street. (keep my eye out for)

Begins with "Get" or "Make"

10 points: If you turn to the right, you will _____. (make a right)

20 points: You need directions because you can't find my house. What happened to you? (You/I got lost.)

30 points: Joe and Bill don't like each other. They don't _____. (get along)

40 points: We should leave now. We should _____. (get going)

50 points: Make a sentence with the idiom "make sure."

Words with "Time"

10 points: If you came to my house at exactly 6:00 P.M., what time did you come? (at 6:00 P.M. sharp)

20 points: It's 3:00 P.M. and Janet has to be at a party at 3:30. She is looking for a present to bring. She is shopping _____. (at the last minute)

30 points: Make a sentence with the idiom "at all times."

40 points: The bus leaves at 12:00 noon and it's now 11:55 A.M. If you want to get to the bus, it will be a _____. (race against time)

50 points: The students should not all try to answer the question together. The students should raise their hands to answer the question

_____. (one at a time)

Glossary

(Number in parentheses indicates lesson number.)

A

	Meaning
a close call (11)	almost a problem/narrow escape
a lemon (5)	defective product
all of a sudden (3)	without warning
as a last resort (11)	if all else fails/as a last choice
as a rule (1)	usually
at all times (8)	always
at first (9)	in the beginning/initially
at the last minute (11)	very late/at the last possible time
at (time) sharp (11)	exactly/promptly at that time

B

back and forth (9)	first one way, then the other
be broke (2)	have no money
believe it or not (5)	it's the truth
by the way (8)	while I think of it

C

call it quits (5)	give up
can't believe one's eyes (9)	very surprised at what one sees
change one's mind (4)	have a new idea or opinion
clear up (1)	explain/fix
come on (4)	say please/encourage someone
count on someone (11)	rely on/depend on
cover a lot of ground (8)	travel over a large area
cut corners (10)	reduce spending/economize

D

drop by (4)	visit

E

early bird special (2)	cheaper price for buying something early

F

feel free to (8)	be comfortable with
feel like (2)	want to
feel sorry for (3)	pity
fill out (1)	complete information on a paper
find one's way around (7)	can easily travel through
find out (2)	get information
for good (10)	permanently

G

get along (10)	live or work well together
get cold feet (10)	become nervous
get going (8)	leave
get in touch with (4)	communicate with
get lost (7)	become lost/lose one's way
give it one's best shot (9)	try one's best

H

hand in (1)	give (to someone)
(not) have a leg to stand on (3)	not have a good story or excuse

I

in advance (1)	before
in charge of (1)	responsible for
in fact (3)	actually
in hot water (9)	have a problem/in trouble
in other words (5)	that is to say
in the mood (4)	feel like/want to

J

jump the gun (3)	start before the correct time

K

keep one's eye out for (7)	look for/watch for
keep on (doing something) (7)	continue
keep one's eye on (9)	watch/take care of
keep up with (8)	go the same speed as

L

lead the way (8)	be the leader
let someone know (10)	tell someone

M

make a note of (1)	write down
make a right (7)	turn right
make up one's mind (2)	decide
make sure (7)	check/be positive

N

no matter what (11)	regardless of anything else
no wonder (10)	it's not surprising

O

one at a time (11)	individually
on its (one's) last legs (5)	in very bad condition
out of the question (2)	impossible

P

pay an arm and a leg (5)	spend a lot of money
pay attention to (3)	look at/listen to carefully
pick up (8)	get or obtain
play it by ear (10)	make decisions as one goes along
pull someone's leg (5)	fool someone
put something off (5)	postpone

R

race against time (9)	something must be finished by a certain time or deadline
right away (3)	immediately
run out of (10)	use up all of something

S

see someone about (11)	check with or ask about
show someone around (8)	give a tour of something
start out (7)	begin

T

take advantage of (5)	make use of something
take a raincheck (4)	ask for another invitation or chance
take care of (1)	give attention to
take it easy (3)	go slowly/relax
take the trouble to (7)	make an effort to
talk someone into something (4)	persuade/convince another person
that makes two of us (2)	I agree
to tell you the truth (2)	honestly
turn someone down (4)	refuse/say no

U

up-to-date (1)	current
up to you (4)	your decision
under the circumstances (11)	because of this/in this situation

W

way ahead of (9)	far in front
well-off (10)	wealthy
win by a mile (9)	take first place easily